D1207427

U.S.-Soviet Summits

An Account of East-West
Diplomacy at the Top,
1955 – 1985

The Institute for the Study of Diplomacy concentrates on the processes of conducting foreign relations abroad, in the belief that diplomatic skills can be taught or improved and that the case study method is useful to that end. Working closely with the academic program of the Georgetown University School of Foreign Service, the Institute conducts a program of publication, teaching, research, conferences and lectures. An associates program enables experienced practitioners of international relations to conduct individual research while sharing their firsthand experience with the university community. Special programs include the junior fellowships in diplomacy, the Dean and Virginia Rusk midcareer fellowship, the Edward Weintal journalism prize, the Jit Trainor diplomacy award, and the Martin F. Herz monograph prize.

U.S.-Soviet Summits

An Account of East-West Diplomacy at the Top, 1955 – 1985

Gordon R. Weihmiller
Epilogue by Dusko Doder

Foreword by David D. Newsom

UNIVERSITY
PRESS OF
AMERICA

LANHAM • NEW YORK • LONDON

INSTITUTE FOR THE
STUDY OF DIPLOMACY

GEORGETOWN UNIVERSITY

Georgetown University
Washington, D.C. 20057

University Press of America,® Inc.

4720 Boston Way
Lanham, MD 20706

3 Henrietta Street
London WC2E 8LU England

Printed in the United States of America

Co-published by arrangement with
the Institute for the Study of Diplomacy,
Georgetown University

Library of Congress Cataloging in Publication Data

Weihmiller, Gordon.
    U.S. Soviet summits.

    Bibliography: p.
    1. United States—Foreign relations—Soviet Union.
2. Soviet Union—Foreign relations—United States.
3. United States—Foreign relations—1945—
4. Soviet Union—Foreign relations—1945—
I. Doder, Dusko. II. Georgetown University.   Institute
for the Study of Diplomacy. III. Title. IV. Title:
Summits.
E183.8.S65W44   1986   327.73047   86-11023
ISBN 0-8191-5442-3 (alk. paper)
ISBN 0-8191-5443-1 (pbk. : alk. paper)

Contents

Foreword

David D. Newsom

W HEN THE QUESTION of an East-West summit meeting has been raised, a standard answer from both sides has been: "We are prepared to meet at the summit, provided adequate preparations are made for such a meeting." This volume seeks to address the question, "What is meant by adequate preparations?"

In this monograph, Gordon R. Weihmiller reviews the preparatory phases of ten meetings that have taken place between leaders of the United States and the Soviet Union since World War II and briefly summarizes the outcome of each. Mr. Weihmiller, a retired Naval officer with A.B. and M.A. degrees, is now a candidate for the Ph.D. degree in the Government Department at Georgetown University. His research and writing for this study were carried out in the winter, spring and summer of 1985, in the midst of which the Reagan-Gorbachev meeting was proposed and set for the coming November in Geneva.

A delay in publication of the study made it possible to incorporate reference to the Geneva summit. Dusko Doder, veteran foreign correspondent for the *Washington Post*, has written an epilogue on the Reagan-Gorbachev meeting. Mr. Doder was Moscow bureau chief for the *Washington*

Post in 1982–85, and served three times as Moscow correspondent, including once with UPI. He has been *Post* correspondent for Eastern Europe and the Mediterranean, the State Department, and Canada, and assistant foreign editor. He is the author of *The Yugoslavs* and is writing a book on the leadership transition in the Soviet political system while on sabbatical from the *Post* at Georgetown University School of Foreign Service during 1985–86.

The project, under the auspices of the Institute for the Study of Diplomacy at Georgetown University, began with the assembly, on March 6, 1985, of a group of those who, in various government positions, had been involved in the preparation of summit meetings. The group included Dr. Madeleine Albright, a member of the National Security Council staff in 1978–81; Lucius D. Battle, Executive Secretary, Department of State, 1948–50; Jacob Beam, U.S. Ambassador to the Soviet Union, 1969–73; Jeanne Davis, Executive Secretary, National Security Council, 1969–76; Mark Garrison, Political Counselor, U.S. Embassy/Moscow, 1971–74, and Director, State Department Office of Soviet Union Affairs, 1974–78; Admiral Thomas H. Moorer (USN-Ret.), Chairman, Joint Chiefs of Staff, 1970–74; Benjamin Read, Executive Secretary, Department of State, 1960–69; and Bromley Smith, member, National Security Council staff, 1952–60. Also in the course of this research, interviews were conducted with Karl D. Ackerman, Deputy Assistant Secretary of State for Security, 1978–81; Dr. I.M. Destler, Senior Fellow, Institute for International Economics; Leslie H. Gelb, Director of the Bureau of Political and Military Affairs, State Department, 1977–79, and Deputy Assistant Secretary of Defense for Policy Planning and Arms Control, 1968–69; Dr. Robert E. Hunter, National Security Council staff member, 1977–81; Dr. Dimitri K. Simes, Senior Associate, Carnegie Endowment for International Peace; William Shinn, Director, Office of Soviet Affairs, State Department, 1977–80; Helmut

Sonnenfeldt, National Security Council staff member, 1969–74, and Counselor, State Department, 1974–77; Peter Tarnoff, Executive Secretary, Department of State, 1976–80; and Malcolm Toon, U.S. Ambassador to the Soviet Union, 1976–79.

In the March 6 meeting and in the interviewing and research, participants have been asked to address the questions of where decisions were made with respect to key aspects of a summit and the degree to which the decisions on the details of preparation may have affected the ultimate outcome. These primary decisions with respect to the meetings' preparations included questions of the timing, the site, security, press, agenda, schedule, attendance, and the drafting of the final communiqué.

The author concentrates on four primary "elements of the process":

1. The timing and circumstances of a decision to hold a summit;
2. Setting the date and location;
3. The issue of preconditions (if any);
4. Setting the agenda.

There are other issues, as well, which, while not highlighted, can be identified as among the decisions that have had to be made in the preparation of at least some of the summit meetings:

1. How to respond to the domestic and foreign pressures for a summit;
2. The division of responsibility within the U.S. bureaucracy for the planning, particularly between the White House and the State Department;
3. The channels through which advance discussions with the Soviets are to take place;
4. The degree of consultation with allies;
5. The preparation of agreements for symbolic signing

at a summit;

6. The problem of record keeping and interpretation at the meetings; and

7. When and at what level the communiqué is to be drafted.

Observations

Out of the meetings, interviews, Mr. Weihmiller's research, and my own experience in the decision-making process, certain observations emerge regarding the preparation of summit meetings and the relationship of the preparatory steps to the policies and successes of the summit:

• There seems never to have been a single point at which the question of whether there should be a summit meeting has been decided. In each administration, the decision appears to have been a matter of the evolution of pressures to the point where a summit became both a diplomatic and a political necessity. With each succeeding administration, the assumption grew that each president would need, at some point, to meet with his Soviet counterpart. The requirement for a summit became absolute.

As one participant in the March meeting stated, "Rarely does someone come from the mountain and say there will be a summit. And equally rarely does there come a question asking: 'Should there be a summit?' Usually it is quite different from that. Usually you begin to see the signs of those elements that make it necessary for the two countries to get together either for their own reasons or collectively. You begin to sense this (pressure) building."

• The move toward a summit is a process including both formal diplomatic contacts between the two sides and "signals." As another participant in the March meeting said, "But don't these (summits) usually start with something less than a direct statement? Generally speaking, don't you get preparation through a series of speeches, a series of lower-level approaches on a subject? . . . It seems to me that it is a matter of floating a statement or picking up one of theirs and saying, 'What did you mean by so and so?' . . . The end of the Berlin blockade, though it wasn't a summit, came from an omission in a Soviet speech of a Soviet phrase that had usually been there. We asked what they had meant by leaving it out. And that led to the meeting in Paris in 1949. . . . (The possibility of a summit) needs to be tested, floated as an idea, a speech made here and there to see what response you get. Domestically, what is the reaction? How do your allies like it, etc.? All of this emerges rather than being direct."

• The preparation of summits has two effects on the policy process. The planning tends to move the center of power to the White House because the president is involved. The fact of the summit creates a deadline that forces decisions on major policy issues—decisions that might otherwise be postponed.

• Summits are domestic political events and the preparation involves as much the development of domestic support as it does the arrangements with the Soviets. In some cases noted by those who had been involved in the process, the mere fact of holding the summit was important politically, regardless of the substance of the meeting itself. As one participant in the Institute's March meeting said of President Johnson (referring to the Glassboro meeting with Kosygin), "I am sure he didn't see any foreign relations aspect to this at all. Everything he did was focused on domestic politics. He thought that would give him a leg up so he was going to run off and see the Russians. When people scurried around to see if they could get some backup material, by that time he was already gone."

• Efforts to prepare for a summit meeting can give an indication of the true interest of the Soviets in having such a meeting. While they may agree in principle, their obstructionist tactics in the preparation phase may well be designed to force the United States to withdraw so the onus of not having a meeting does not fall on them. One participant in the March meeting, discussing the preparation of the agenda, said, "I think the difficulty arises only in terms of the intentions of the two parties. A related experience was in 1950 when we tried to negotiate an agenda for a foreign ministers' conference. We spent six weeks in the damndest performance ever that I experienced. Other than being in Paris, it was a hideous experience. It broke up with no agreement on an agenda for a foreign ministers' meeting. So it was obvious the Russians did not want to meet and they were just carrying out a commitment."

• The ceremonial aspects—the toasts, the speeches, the wreath layings—are all part of the substance of a summit meeting and often involve as much advance negotiation and preparation as the issues of the meetings themselves.

• It is symbolic of the course of global politics that, while summit meetings before 1960 were multilateral discussions that included the principal U.S. allies, all of those since have been bilateral meetings emphasizing concrete agreements. Consultations with allies has taken place, but such consultations appear to be less and less central to the decisions and substance regarding a U.S.-Soviet summit. The trend of the summit meetings has also moved from an initial emphasis on multiple international problems to a later emphasis on strategic nuclear weapons.

• Each president has questioned the value of a summit and few have been enthusiastic. Those summit meetings deemed most successful at the time, such as the Vladivostok meeting in 1974 between President Ford and General Secretary Brezhnev, have been the climax of a negotiation over a significant bilateral agreement.

• Summits are always at the peril of events, such as the shooting down of the U-2 on the eve of a planned Paris summit in 1960, although, as the bombing of Haiphong on the eve of the Nixon-Brezhnev summit of 1972 demonstrated, hard-line actions on the part of the United States do not scuttle such meetings if the desire to hold them is sufficiently strong on the part of the Soviets.

A full account of the preparation for summit meetings and the implications of that preparation for the success of the meeting would require an examination of the Soviet side of the preparation. With the exception of a few published sources quoted in Mr. Weihmiller's paper, it was not possible to develop additional material on this important aspect. Other aspects that merit further examination if one is to have a complete picture of the process of preparation would include: the advance press arrangements, security arrangements, the decision on attendance at the meetings, and the drafting of the communiqué.

Summary information on each summit and the final communiqués or statements are included as an appendix to this volume.

The Institute is indebted to the J. Howard Pew Freedom Trust for funding for this project and to the Institute's editor, Margery R. Boichel, who worked with the manuscript and the publisher to bring the book to publication in the relatively brief time available.

1

Arranging U.S.-Soviet Summits

Since the days when President Wilson made his European trips to participate in the formulation of the Treaty of Versailles, many conflicting opinions have been expressed, most often in generalities, as to the wisdom of a President of the United States meeting personally with other heads of government. It seems to me that conclusions of this kind rarely have value if they are meant to apply universally and eternally; each set of circumstances has to provide the answer.

—Dwight D. Eisenhower, *The White House Years*[1]

Getting to Geneva, November 1985

THREE AND A HALF hours after the announcement from Moscow on Monday, March 11, 1985 of Konstantin Chernenko's death the previous evening, President Reagan conferred in the Oval Office with his top aides, including Secretary of State George Shultz and National Security Adviser Robert McFarlane. The subject of discussion was the advisability of a presidential trip to Moscow to attend Chernenko's funeral and meet the new general secretary of

---

[1]Dwight D. Eisenhower, *The White House Years: Mandate for Change, 1953–1956* (Garden City, N.Y.: Doubleday & Co., 1963), p. 503.

the Central Committee of the Communist Party of the Soviet Union, Mikhail Gorbachev. It was already known that most of the other Western leaders would attend. The president was urged by his foreign policy advisers to make the trip as a gesture of goodwill toward the Soviets at a critical time in superpower relations. The meeting with Gorbachev, the third new Soviet leader in less than two and a half years, would provide the occasion for an impromptu summit, and Secretary Shultz weighed the pros and cons of that eventuality.[2] Surely some discussion focused on the hope of initiating a fresh break in the decline and general malaise of U.S.-Soviet relations during recent years.

Having considered the arguments for and against a trip to Moscow, the president announced his decision: he would not attend Chernenko's funeral. His mind was already made up; based on an earlier meeting with Donald Regan, White House Chief of Staff, and Michael Deaver, it was decided that he should not go, reportedly "because there was insufficient time to prepare for a meeting with Gorbachev and little prospect of fulfilling the high expectations such a trip would inevitably create."[3] The alternative accepted was to send Vice President George Bush to head the U.S. delegation at the funeral ceremonies as he had previously upon the deaths of Yuri Andropov in February 1984 and Leonid Brezhnev in November 1982. But there was to be a difference this time—Chernenko's death would give birth to a summit.

The president equipped Bush with a "personal message" to the new Soviet leader, inviting him to meet with the president at a mutually convenient time. The vice president was further instructed to discuss the possibilities of such a meeting with the general secretary if he had the opportunity. Later in the day, Reagan told reporters that he was

---

[2]"Ending an Era of Drift," *Time* (March 25, 1985), p. 17.
[3]Ibid.

"more than ready" for a meeting with Gorbachev once the new Soviet leader was settled in and could "establish his regime."[4] Additional evidence that his invitation was something more than a gesture of good will was found by the press in the apparent omission of any reference to the president's previously held "preconditions" for a summit meeting with his Soviet counterpart.[5] The pieces were beginning to fit together—as Mikhail Gorbachev was preparing to lay his predecessor to rest behind the Lenin Mausoleum, the president was shifting his hard-line stance on the "evil empire."

Following the military procession in Red Square and Chernenko's interment on March 13, General Secretary Gorbachev, accompanied by Prime Minister Nikolai Tikhonov, First Vice President Vasily Kuznetsov and Foreign Minister Andrei Gromyko, hosted a reception in St. George's Hall in the Kremlin for the scores of foreign dignitaries attending the funeral. There Gorbachev greeted Vice President Bush and Secretary Shultz along with numerous world leaders that included British Prime Minister Margaret Thatcher, French President François Mitterrand, West German Chancellor Helmut Kohl, Japanese Prime Minister Yasuhiro Nakasone, Indian Prime Minister Rajiv Gandhi and Chinese Vice Premier Li Peng.[6] He then launched into a series of private meetings with many of the leaders that lasted for more than fifteen hours spaced over the next few days.

Bush and Shultz met privately with Gorbachev and Gromyko for nearly an hour and a half on the first day, at

---

[4]"President Sends an Invitation to Gorbachev for Summit," *Washington Post* (March 13, 1985), pp. A1 and A26.

[5]As established during President Reagan's first administration, these standing requirements for any serious consideration of a summit meeting had included insistence on adequate preparations, reasonable chances for success and, at one point, that the Soviets improve their international behavior. Ibid., p. A26.

[6]Among the Soviet bloc and Third World leaders, conspicuously absent was Cuba's President Fidel Castro and conspicuously present, in U.S. press accounts at least, was Nicaraguan President Daniel Ortega.

which time they conveyed President Reagan's personal message as well as his hopes for improved relations with the Soviet Union. Although the vice president did not say publicly what Gorbachev's response to the invitation had been, he did express a relatively optimistic account of their meeting.[7] White House officials later characterized Gorbachev's response as "we are interested and we will get back to you."[8] By the end of the week, the Soviet news agency Tass reported that Gorbachev had accepted, in principle, invitations to visit President Mitterrand and Chancellor Kohl, but there was no announcement concerning President Reagan's invitation.

What followed may have been a somewhat uncomfortable delay for the president in waiting for Moscow's response. In a nationally televised news conference on March 21 Reagan had to fend off a reporter's question about being "rebuffed" to date by Gorbachev's lack of acceptance.[9] Later, in an interview with the *Washington Post* on April 1, the president said that a reply from Gorbachev had been received recently and it was considered positive by some, although he admitted that it was vague and noncommittal. White House spokesman Larry Speakes added: "There has been no discussion about arrangements for a summit, no meeting set, no time set, nothing along those lines."[10] Then, on April 10, House Speaker Thomas P. O'Neill and a small number of visiting U.S. congressmen met with Gorbachev for four hours in the Kremlin and delivered a second letter from the president reaffirming his interest in a meeting. Gorbachev, while indicating that he

---

[7]"Moscow Buries Third Ruler in Less Than 2½ Years" and "Bush Is Optimistic after Talks with Gorbachev," *Washington Post* (March 14, 1985), pp. A1 and A27 respectively.

[8]"Ending an Era of Drift," *Time* op. cit., p. 18.

[9]"Text of President Reagan's News Conference," *Washington Post* (March 22, 1985), p. A18.

[10]Quoted in "A Tentative RSVP from Moscow," *Time* (April 15, 1985), p. 72.

was amenable to such a meeting, again was not specific about his intentions.[11]

By mid-April White House officials began to distinguish between a summit meeting with Gorbachev and a "get-acquainted" session between the two leaders, adding that the president favored the latter and that an opportunity for this might be found in the fall when the new general secretary might visit the United Nations for the opening session of the General Assembly. A more formal summit meeting, they said, could then be arranged to follow these preliminary talks.[12] Perhaps, at the time, the distinction was drawn as a means of inducing a more forthright acceptance from Gorbachev of the president's proposal for a meeting, although some differences of opinion about the purpose of their initial contact had already begun to surface in Washington. For example, White House Chief of Staff Donald Regan was reported as saying that the president was against "just having meetings for meetings' sake" and "we think it would be a big letdown ... if the two leaders were to meet and accomplish nothing."[13] National Security Adviser McFarlane was also reported as "edging away from the notion of a precooked summit" and said the purpose of the meeting was "to get to know each other ... and assess each other's commitment to the resolution of problems."[14] Secretary of State Shultz was quoted as saying: "My opinion is that a pure-and-simple get-acquainted session is not the way to go."[15]

Although Viktor Afanasyev, editor of the Communist Party newspaper *Pravda*, told the Reuters news agency on

---

[11]"Up in the Air after Moscow's Gambit," *Time* (April 22, 1985), p. 13.

[12]"Gorbachev Assails Speed of U.S. Reply to Missile Freeze, President Clarifies Position on Summit," *Washington Post* (April 11, 1985), pp. A1, A28.

[13]*Time* (April 22, 1985), op. cit.

[14]Ibid.

[15]"U.S. Begins Work on Summit Agenda," *Washington Post* (April 5, 1985), p. A11.

April 22 in Moscow that Gorbachev would attend the United Nations session in the fall and might well meet with Reagan at that time, there was no official confirmation of that report from Moscow.[16]

Speculation in Washington continued to mount for the next several weeks: What was the cause for the delay in setting a date and place for the Reagan-Gorbachev meeting? Was the new leader preoccupied with getting his house in order, or were both leaders beginning to play their summit cards more closely to the chest?

In mid-May Secretary Shultz and Foreign Minister Gromyko met in Vienna where dignitaries had gathered to observe the thirtieth anniversary of the Austrian State Treaty. In anticipation that their meeting might produce an accord on the Reagan-Gorbachev summit, National Security Adviser McFarlane readied some new suggestions for progress on arms control talks, which had been deadlocked in Geneva for six weeks and were currently in recess, and accompanied Shultz. It was reported that Shultz would put forth the suggestions if the Soviets accepted Reagan's proposal for a summit meeting.[17] But after six hours of talks with Gromyko on May 14, Shultz found no new prospects for the summit and McFarlane had to keep the proposals in his pocket. The message from Vienna was clear: Gorbachev was not ready to address plans for meeting with the president.

Shortly after that meeting, on May 16, Shultz and McFarlane briefed the president, and Larry Speakes told reporters that Reagan's invitation was for Gorbachev to come to Washington, not to the United Nations. "Any location other than the one in the invitation originally extended has not been addressed by this administration,"

---

[16]"Gorbachev Unlikely to Go to U.N. Session This Fall," *Washington Post* (May 21, 1985), p. A1.

[17]Joseph Kraft (editorial) "The Big Two Mark Time," *Washington Post* (May 21, 1985), p. A19.

Speakes added.[18] Sensitivities about further delays in setting the date and place for the summit meeting were, evidently, becoming more strained.

A full month passed without any visible progress on arrangements for the meeting. In the latter part of June, Armand Hammer, chairman of Occidental Petroleum Corporation and a frequent visitor to Moscow, met with Gorbachev for an hour and a half and said that he had been told by Soviet Ambassador Anatoliy F. Dobrynin that the Soviet leader would not be attending the United Nations session in the fall. On June 21, White House officials confirmed that report. Then, somewhat unexpectedly, a week later, diplomatic sources in Moscow (otherwise unidentified in the press) announced that tentative agreement had been reached to hold the meeting in Geneva in the latter half of November.[19] On July 2, White House officials confirmed the summit date as set for November 19th to 21st and stated that this had been established earlier in the week by State Department discussions with Ambassador Dobrynin.[20]

At the end of July Secretary Shultz met for three hours in Helsinki with the newly-appointed Soviet Foreign Minister, Eduard Shevardnadze, while attending the commemoration of the tenth anniversary of the signing of the Final Act of the Conference on Security and Cooperation in Europe (CSCE). Shultz said the talks constituted "a good first step" toward reaching agreement on an agenda for the November summit meeting, but cautioned that "very deep differences" remained on many issues. Reportedly, both sides agreed on three broad agenda items: arms control,

---

[18]Quoted in "Gorbachev Not Ready to Discuss Top-Level Meeting, Reagan Is Told," *Washington Post* (May 17, 1985), p. A26.

[19]"Tentative Accord Set on Fall Summit Site," *Washington Post* (June 29, 1985), p. A1.

[20]"Reagan-Gorbachev Meeting Set for Nov. 19-21 in Geneva," *Washington Post* (July 3, 1985), p. A1.

points of regional conflict, and bilateral issues. Strong disagreement arose over the U.S. proposal to include human rights in the agenda. Soviet Foreign Ministry spokesman Vladimir Lomeiko said that Shevardnadze had "pointed out the inadmissibility of interference in the [internal] affairs of other states" when this was broached in their talks.[21]

Elements of the Process

THE FOREGOING SEQUENCE of events paving the way to the Reagan-Gorbachev meeting in Geneva illustrates a number of concerns that have previously arisen in the process of arranging and preparing for the ten U.S.-Soviet summits held from 1955 in Geneva to 1979 in Vienna. At this point, it may be useful to identify certain aspects of the process in the Reagan-Gorbachev summit arrangements that will serve as points of observation and comparison in the following chapters, and to identify the purposes for which this study is undertaken as well.

TIMING. One important element—a sense of timing—seems critical to the determination by a president of when a summit meeting with his Soviet counterpart would be in the national interest, as well as when it would favor his domestic standing and international prestige. The stakes are simply too high and the consequences of failure too great for the president not to apply his finest political acuity to the timing of a summit initiative, whether it be a U.S. proposal or a response to a Soviet proposal.

In the preceding narrative of the Reagan-Gorbachev maneuvering, timing appears to have been an important

---

[21]"Shultz Terms Soviet Talks 'Good First Step,' " *Washington Post* (August 1, 1985), p. A25.

consideration in both leaders' plans and motivations, at least to the extent that can be observed in the public record to date. The president's invitation to Gorbachev immediately followed Chernenko's death. It may well be that the accession of the markedly younger leader, aged 54, signaled to the president a positive change in Politburo practices that he saw as encouraging for improvements in U.S.-Soviet relations. Gorbachev had projected a new image to the West during his previous visit to London, where Prime Minister Thatcher's favorable comments were closely observed by those concerned with the prospect of the next succession in Soviet leadership. He was seen as "a man with whom we could conduct business." His Western dress and demeanor accentuated the contrasts with the aging and infirm Chernenko and his predecessors. In short, presented with an opportunity for a change in the stagnated state of U.S.-Soviet relations, the president seized the moment.

But the timing was also advantageous to President Reagan for a number of other reasons, foremost of which was that he could make the proposal from a position of strength. Not only did he have the experience of a successful first administration behind him, but the president also enjoyed the confidence and support of the American public, as evidenced in his 1984 landslide reelection. As he comfortably settled in to his second term, the prior increases in national defense spending and his hard-line reputation underscored the image of a strong and confident president fully capable of presenting a formidable challenge at a conference table confronting a newly-appointed Soviet leader. When President Reagan made the proposal, then, he was clearly dealing from strength and it was timed to his advantage. Chernenko's death and the new face in the Kremlin provided the opportunity.

But perhaps this was all too evident in Moscow as well. If so, it could account for the initial hesitancy and subsequent caution displayed by Gorbachev in not responding to the president's invitation, even "in principle" as he had done in responding to those of President Mitterrand and Chancellor Kohl. If it is almost axiomatic that world leaders need to be perceived as being "in control" of their own countries when negotiating at the conference table, then Gorbachev's first task prerequisite to acceptance of the proposed summit was to establish his own credentials and put his house in order.

This he did in dramatic fashion in the succeeding months. Grigory Romanov, who was widely perceived in the West as Gorbachev's chief rival in the succession of power, was relieved of his duties in the Politburo on July 1, and Eduard Shevardnadze was elected to full membership in that body, joining three other Gorbachev supporters elected in April. On the following day, Gorbachev nominated 28-year veteran Foreign Minister Gromyko to be president, or, more formally, chairman of the Presidium of the Supreme Soviet. After Gromyko was elected, Gorbachev immediately announced that Eduard Shevardnadze would replace him as foreign minister. The signals from Moscow were unmistakable: Gorbachev was in charge and intended to be the indisputable master of Soviet foreign policy. The changes positioned him well for his November summit meeting with President Reagan, and the date and location of the meeting were finally settled and announced that same week.

CIRCUMSTANCES. To say that a shrewd sense of timing is an important aspect of U.S.-Soviet summitry adds little to what one might expect of experienced leaders whose political fortunes necessarily require a fine appreciation of opportune maneuvers. Judgments about timing are intertwined with circumstance, and the context in which summit planning unfolds is part and parcel of the process. At the outset of this chapter, President Eisenhower is quoted suggesting that the wisdom of meeting with foreign leaders depended on the specific set of circumstances under which each meeting took place.

At the time of the White House announcement in March of President Reagan's invitation to Gorbachev, spokesman Larry Speakes alluded to improvements in the "atmospherics" of U.S.-Soviet relations, and one could point to some (admittedly few) changes for the better in recent times.[22] The president had met with Politburo member Vladimir Shcherbitsky earlier in the month; his first meeting with Foreign Minister Gromyko had occurred the previous September. Strategic nuclear arms reduction talks were resuming with the Soviets in Geneva and the president seemed to be displaying a different tone in his remarks about the Soviet Union. Perhaps the election rhetoric about his being the first president since Herbert Hoover not to meet with the leader of the Soviet Union during his presidency contributed to the change in his disposition. And he was no doubt further encouraged in his efforts by a "sense of the Senate" resolution, passed by a vote of 84 to 10 on May 21, 1985, urging that his meeting with Gorbachev be arranged "at the earliest possible time."

SETTING THE DATE. Timing and circumstance influence not only the decisions to propose and to accept the holding of a summit meeting, but also the selection of a meeting date. It is reasonable to assume that both the Soviets and the U.S. will want a sufficient period between agreement to meet and the date of the meeting itself so as to permit attempts to influence the international atmosphere in the interim. Several observations can be made here to illustrate the point.

First, it took almost four full months from the date of President Reagan's proposal to Gorbachev's agreement on where and when the summit meeting would occur. That

---

[22]"President Sends an Invitation to Gorbachev for Summit," *Washington Post* (March 13, 1985), p. A26.

would appear entirely a matter of practicality, considering that the new Soviet leader had to "establish his regime," as the president remarked. But he not only established himself and asserted his control of Soviet affairs, he also set into motion some initiatives that bore a relationship to the November meeting. The announcement that he would visit Paris and meet with President Mitterrand on October 2 to 5—a full month before meeting with the president of the United States—conveyed an impression of a rearrangement of Soviet foreign policy priorities.

His unilateral announcement on April 7 that the Soviet Union was placing a moratorium on further deployment of SS-20 missiles targeted on Europe was timed to expire a few days before the November summit. Certainly this put the issue of further U.S. deployments of medium-range missiles to the NATO allies back in the spotlight again, particularly so for the Dutch government, set to decide in November if it would accept forty-eight U.S. cruise missiles or not.[23] Adding further pressures on the president prior to the summit, Gorbachev announced a unilateral moratorium on nuclear testing on July 30, a measure that was quickly rejected in Washington as a public relations gambit. The Soviet moratorium was set to extend through the November summit and thus to focus attention on the U.S. refusal to join in the test ban. In short, both the timing and the circumstances of a summit can be manipulated to advantage.

LOCATION. Another aspect of summit planning concerns agreement on the location of the meeting. Although the president's invitation to meet referred to a mutually convenient time, the location was clearly intended to be Washington. As the president later remarked at his press

---

[23]Jim Hoagland (editorial), "Gorbachev's Summit Plot: Leave Egg on Reagan's Face," *Washington Post* (August 11, 1985), p. L2.

conference on March 21, "It's our turn to be the hosts."[24] The most recent prior U.S.-Soviet summit, President Carter's meeting with General Secretary Brezhnev in June 1979, had been in Vienna, which is considered "neutral" territory; but the two preceding meetings were on Soviet territory: President Ford's meeting with Brezhnev at Vladivostok in November 1974 and the Nixon-Brezhnev summit in Moscow in June and July of the same year. Therefore, if there is a protocol to be observed, reciprocity would call for a location in the United States.

In May, however, Gorbachev let it be known informally that he was "too busy" for such a trip and suggested that Reagan come to Moscow. The president declined and suggested that he would be willing to go to Moscow for a second summit meeting if Gorbachev came to Washington first.[25] The standoff on location continued with alternative sites proposed in Helsinki or Vienna, as favored by Gorbachev, or Geneva, as favored by Reagan. Meeting in Helsinki with the Soviet leader might convey the wrong impression, since the U.S. has accused the Soviets of ignoring important provisions of the accords signed there in 1975. And while Vienna was more acceptable, Reagan preferred Geneva, possibly to underscore his opposition to the SALT II treaty signed at the former location by President Carter. It was not until July 1 that the Soviets agreed to Geneva, as reported then by Ambassador Dobrynin to Secretary Shultz. With this agreement on a "neutral" site, some speculation arose as to whether President Reagan was showing overeagerness for the summit by relinquishing a possible point of protocol favoring a U.S. location for the meeting.

---

[24]"Text of President's News Conference," *Washington Post* (March 22, 1985), p. A18.

[25]"Reagan Offered to Hold Two Summits with Gorbachev," *Washington Post* (July 4, 1985), p. A29.

PRECONDITIONS. Another element in the process that merits attention concerns the role of preconditions. As already noted, the president omitted reference to his former requirements for a summit meeting when he issued the invitation to the new Soviet leader. The question arises as to why. Considering the high stakes of summit diplomacy and the historical record, the use of preconditions has not been an unusual mechanism to help ensure success at the summit, however that may be defined, or to block such an occurrence when a meeting is not desired for any number of reasons.

The deletion of standing requirements, then, effectively implies the willingness to meet one's counterpart without any prior evidence of good intentions. It is, thus, both an inducement to meet and a tacit acceptance of an equal footing for the leaders. Whether the lack of a summit meeting with Gorbachev's predecessors is attributable more to Reagan's preconditions or to fate is problematical, but their deletion in his invitation to the new leader clearly conveyed a positive signal to Moscow.

AGENDA. The final aspect of the process that will be discussed in the following chapters concerns the agenda and how it is determined. While agreement on the date and location for the November 1985 summit arose well prior to initiation of discussions on its substantive content, this does not imply any judgement about their respective importance. Setting the date and site first is at times only a practical necessity, considering the vast amount of administrative and logistical planning that is required in advance of a summit.

The meetings between Secretary Shultz and Foreign Minister Shevardnadze in Helsinki on July 30, 1985 reportedly reached agreement on three agenda items for the November summit: 1) arms control and security, 2) regional conflicts such as Afghanistan, Kampuchea and Central America, and 3) bilateral matters, including trade and cultural exchanges. These have become the traditional agenda items for high-level U.S.-Soviet meetings in recent years. A fourth item, human rights, appeared on the U.S. list but not the Soviet one.[26]

* * *

Primary attention in this survey of the ten previous postwar summits, then, will be given to these considerations: timing and circumstance, setting the date and location, the role of preconditions (if any), and the setting of the agenda. Other aspects of summit preparations—the pressures presidents experience that tend to push them toward summit meetings, the influence of public expectations and domestic political concerns, the role of the media and public relations, and the international context—will also be discussed in places. The goal is to examine the mechanics of the process itself, not the substance of the issues at stake.

This is not to imply that it is either possible or wise to separate process from policy when it comes to the matter of preparations, but only to circumscribe the more limited objectives in the present study. After surveying the historical record of the postwar U.S.-Soviet summits, it will be possible to compare the processes involved in arranging and preparing for these meetings and to draw some conclusions.

---

[26]"Taking the First Step," *Time* (August 12, 1985), p. 25.

2

The Eisenhower-
Khrushchev Summits

The Geneva Conference of Heads of
Government, July 18–23, 1955

THE EARLIEST MOVEMENT among the Western allies in the
postwar years toward convening a summit conference
with the Soviets can be traced to an address by Prime
Minister Churchill before the House of Commons on May
11, 1953 shortly after Joseph Stalin's death, in which he
called for diplomacy at the "summit."[1] "Another talk with
Soviet Russia upon the highest level" was now required, he
said, adding that it would be a mistake "to assume that
nothing can be settled with Soviet Russia unless or until
everything is settled."[2] Mistaken or not, however, this
opinion was not shared in the United States, where the
Cold War had produced stiff resistance to the idea of sitting
down at the conference table with Soviet leaders. Harry

---

[1]Elmer Plischke, ed., *Modern Diplomacy: The Art and the Artisans* (Washington, D.C.: American Enterprise Institute for Public Policy Research, 1979), p. 170.

[2]House of Commons, *Parliamentary Debates*, Fifth Series, Vol. 515, Cols. 883-98, as cited in Keith Eubank, *The Summit Conferences 1919-1960* (Norman, Oklahoma: University of Oklahoma Press, 1966), pp. 136-37.

Truman had put the matter bluntly in 1948 at the time of the first Berlin crisis:

> There is nothing to negotiate when one nation disregards the principles of international conduct to which all members of the United Nations subscribed. There is nothing to negotiate when one nation habitually uses coercion and open aggression in international affairs.[3]

The onset of the Cold War gave rise to a set of four basic requirements by the United States for tangible evidence of better intentions on the part of Soviet leaders before any such meeting would receive serious attention. These requirements, or preconditions as they became commonly called, generally specified the following: 1) abandonment of the Marxist principle of world revolution, 2) cessation of aggressive action, 3) adherence to the principles of the United Nations Charter, and 4) fulfillment of international agreements.[4]

In his memoirs, President Eisenhower recalled his thoughts about summits:

> Few of my associates urged me to seek a "Summit"; indeed, almost without exception they were opposed to the idea. Their skepticism was based on the dim prospects of useful results in view of Communist intransigence. Secretary Dulles, in particular, was emphatically of this view.... I developed a stock answer to any question about a possible summit. "I would not go to a Summit merely because of friendly words and plausible promises by the men in the Kremlin; actual deeds giving some indication of a Communist readiness to negotiate constructively will have to be produced before I would agree to such a meeting."[5]

---

[3]U.S. Department of State, *Bulletin*, Vol. 18 (June 20, 1948), p. 805, as cited in Elmer Plischke, *Summit Diplomacy: Personal Diplomacy of the President of the United States* (College Park: University of Maryland, 1958), p. 81.

[4]Plischke, *Summit Diplomacy*, p. 82.

[5]Eisenhower, *Mandate for Change*, pp. 504-5.

Although this indeed became his stock answer to questions about a summit meeting, Emmet John Hughes has quoted Eisenhower in a more direct statement of his feelings to a cabinet meeting on July 17, 1953: "This idea of the President of the United States going personally abroad to negotiate—it's just damn stupid. Every time a President has gone abroad to get into the details of these things, he's lost his shirt."[6] Dulles' own misgivings centered on his projections of Soviet purposes at a summit: 1) to popularize the notion that Moscow's intentions were pacific, 2) to minimize the chance of war while the Soviet Union rebuilt its strength, and 3) to bring about a relaxation not of tensions, but rather of Western strength and unity.[7]

But with the passage of time, starting after the truce in the Korean War of July 1953, Eisenhower's resistance to a summit meeting with the Soviets came under increasing pressures from the allies. In April of 1954, Churchill tried without success to convert the president and Dulles at their meeting in Bermuda. The following November, French Premier Pierre Mendès-France spoke before the United Nations and called for a four-power meeting in Paris. This was rejected by Eisenhower because he demanded adequate preparations by the foreign ministers before he would consider the prospect of a summit and because the Paris Agreements accepting West Germany into NATO had not yet been ratified.[8]

Also in November 1954, the Soviets convened a security conference in Moscow attended by the Eastern bloc

---

[6]Emmet John Hughes, *The Ordeal of Power* (New York: Atheneum, 1963), p. 151.

[7]W.W. Rostow, *The United States in the World Arena* (New York: Harper & Row, 1960), p. 347.

[8]The French National Assembly had rejected a treaty for the European Defense Community in August 1954, but following the warnings of Dulles' "agonizing reappraisal" reversed that decision in October and agreed to West Germany's joining of NATO. This represented a major failure of Soviet efforts to prevent German rearmament and entry into NATO.

countries. Then, in early December, they announced that they would form a counterpart to NATO if the Paris Agreements were ratified. But with that ratification assured by the following March (1955), the chairman of the Senate Foreign Relations Committee, Walter F. George, publicly began to advocate a four-power conference. The pressure on Eisenhower increased markedly when the Soviets, faced with the reality of West German independence on May 5, 1955, undertook a new diplomatic initiative. They invited Chancellor Konrad Adenauer to Moscow, announced plans to seek a rapprochement with Yugoslavia, and, most importantly, concluded and signed the Austrian State Treaty on May 15. It was the imminence of the latter event, more than any other, that finally persuaded Eisenhower to give in to the pressures for a summit. He wrote:

> Because of the Soviet's action, and not wishing to appear senselessly stubborn in my attitude toward a Summit meeting—so hopefully desired by so many—I instructed Secretary Dulles to let it be known through diplomatic channels, that if other powers were genuinely interested in such a meeting we were ready to listen to their reasoning.[9]

As for the allies, Sir Anthony Eden, who had replaced Churchill as prime minister, reversed his earlier opposition to the idea of a summit meeting and promptly became a

---

[9]Eisenhower, *Mandate for Change* p. 506. Eisenhower later wrote the following to his lifelong friend Everett E. ("Swede") Hazlett on August 15, 1955: "My reactions to Geneva have been fairly well publicized. It was difficult indeed to reach a decision that I should go to such a meeting. The twin dangers of encouraging complacency or defeatism, depending upon the outcome, were very great indeed. These, however, were lessened by the Soviet agreement to the Austrian Treaty, by their invitation to Adenauer to come to Moscow—after having previously threatened the most dire consequences in the event that the Paris Agreements (formally approving the inclusion of West Germany into NATO) were signed—and finally the general attitude of the new Kremlin masters: all of these encouraged the belief that possibly a new attitude might be developed in the conduct of foreign relations." *Ike's Letters to a Friend, 1941–1958*, ed. Robert Griffith (Lawrence: University Press of Kansas, 1984), pp. 149–50.

vociferous advocate, possibly because he needed the public exposure it would provide.[10] French Premier Edgar Faure also came under pressure, mostly from the left wing, to take a conciliatory approach toward Moscow. After a meeting of the three Western powers, a tripartite note was issued to the Soviets on May 10, 1955 inviting them to a conference "in an effort to remove the sources of conflict between us." The note suggested that the purpose of the meeting was to formulate the issues in "an exchange of views," but "not [to] undertake to agree upon substantive answers to the major difficulties facing the world."[11]

Meeting in Vienna on the 15th of May for the signing of the Austrian State Treaty, Foreign Minister Vyacheslav Molotov informed his Western counterparts of Moscow's favorable reaction to the proposed conference. This was confirmed officially in a Soviet note of May 26. Another exchange of notes, completed on June 13, agreed upon Geneva as the conference site, with the meeting to begin on July 18. The Soviet note of acceptance further stated: "In the present situation, the efforts of the Governments of all Four Powers participating in the conference should be directed first of all to guaranteeing the fulfillment of the basic task of the conference—reducing tension in international relations."[12]

Another meeting with Molotov took place in New York in mid-June and was followed later in the month by more discussions among the foreign ministers in San Francisco, where they had gathered to observe the tenth anniversary of the signing of the United Nations Charter. These meetings were of the preparatory type that Eisenhower had insisted on for so long. While general agreement was

---

[10]Jacob Beam, *Multiple Exposure* (New York: W.W. Norton & Co., 1978), p. 43.
   [11]U.S. Department of State, *Bulletin*, Vol. 32, No. 830 (May 23, 1955), pp. 832-33.
   [12]U.S. Department of State, *Bulletin*, Vol. 33, No. 836 (July 4, 1955), p. 21.

reached on the procedures to follow at the summit conference, differences on agenda items were not resolved. Dulles proposed to define the issues as disarmament, German unification, European security, and the goals of international communism. Molotov was amenable to including disarmament and European security and added economic cooperation, but the differences arose out of the priorities accorded the subjects. For the West in general and the U.S. in particular, German reunification was to be the first order of business; but Molotov would only agree to that if it were subsumed in a discussion of European security.

In terms of internal preparations for the conference, Eisenhower's approach was thorough and intensive, and required great coordination with the allies. His conception of proper preparation presents a paradigm of the process:

> A full-scale international conference involves difficult and intricate preparation by each participating government. "Position papers"—documents on all conceivable issues, setting forth the position the government intends to present at the meeting—have to be carefully written and approved. Responsible United States officials have to reach agreements with their opposite numbers in other governments about the schedules of meetings, agenda, details of timing, and personnel to be present in the conference room, while advance parties from each country must go to the selected spot to make arrangements for offices and living accommodations, communications, handling of the press, and security. Social activities must be coordinated; even the matter of the exchange of gifts, when this appears appropriate—in this case it did not apply—involves sensitive advance planning.[13]

In the State Department, a preparatory group had already been set up in April headed by counselor Douglas

---

[13]Eisenhower, *Mandate for Change*, pp. 506-7.

MacArthur II, who oversaw coordination with Congress and the other government agencies. Jacob Beam, his deputy, became the principal point of contact with the allies. Three groups were set up, corresponding to the expected agenda: the first to handle political and international security affairs, the second for disarmament, and the third for economic and cultural exchanges between East and West.[14] Most of the coordination with NATO foreign ministers was done in Paris, although Secretary Dulles also met frequently with Chancellor Adenauer in Bonn.

By any measure, the coordination effort among the allies was extensive and thorough. Prior to his arrival in Geneva, Dulles met with the French and British foreign ministers in Paris to review the results of a report that had been assembled by a working group and then attended the council meeting of the North Atlantic Treaty Organization for further discussions with representatives of the fifteen member countries. Upon his departure, Secretary Dulles observed:

> There is every reason to believe that the three Western powers see eye to eye with reference to the matters which are likely to come up at Geneva. This initial unity is a good beginning of our efforts to reach agreement with the Soviet Union on the stated purpose of the Geneva conference, namely to identify the issues to be worked on in the future and to agree on the international procedures to be established for finding solutions.
>
> The Geneva conference will be a beginning and not an end. It is not expected that great decisions of substance will be made there.[15]

America's Ambassador in Moscow, Charles E. Bohlen, saw the conference as an opportunity to gain valuable insights into Soviet thinking. On June 12 he sent a lengthy

---

[14]Beam, *Multiple Exposure*, p. 43.
[15]U.S. Department of State, *Bulletin*, Vol. 33, No. 839 (July 25, 1955), p. 132.

dispatch emphasizing Soviet preoccupation with two main objectives: retention of control over their East European satellites and avoidance of war with the West.[16] He pointed out a change in the Kremlin's attitude toward a relaxation of tensions, noting that the arms race was straining the Soviet economy, that the Soviets would not permit atomic inspections, and that they would try to dismantle NATO.

Further projections about Soviet intentions at Geneva were gained from a special study group, set up under presidential aide Nelson A. Rockefeller, which met in Quantico, Virginia from June 5 through June 10. That group, which later became known as the Quantico Panel, was composed of eleven senior officials who were to take stock of where the United States stood in world affairs and to recommend courses of action for the president at the summit.[17] The Quantico Panel was responsible for what later was known as Eisenhower's "Open Skies" proposal at Geneva, and saw it as a test of Soviet intentions, particularly with regard to U.S. insistence on adequate inspection guarantees for any disarmament proposals.

By the time Eisenhower was ready to depart for the conference in Geneva, he had received 20 basic documents, prepared for him by the State Department, and more than 150 secondary papers. His objective was focused on "defining crucial world problems" at the summit that would then be delegated to the foreign ministers for subsequent negotiations. In a national broadcast before his departure, he stated his conviction that "our many postwar conferences have been characterized by too much attention to details—by an effort apparently to work on specific

[16]Charles E. Bohlen, *Witness to History* (New York: W.W. Norton & Co., 1973), p. 381.

[17]W.W. Rostow, *Open Skies: Eisenhower's Proposal of July 21, 1955* (Austin: University of Texas Press, 1982), p. 26.

problems rather than establish the spirit and attitude in which we should approach them."[18]

While the allies accepted Eisenhower's purposes, there remained, nonetheless, a measure of disunity on substantive priorities, and there was no unified plan of action for the conference.[19] Nor had all the agenda issues been resolved with the Soviets prior to the start of the conference. Because of this the foreign ministers had to assemble in the mornings to develop agenda schedules for the day's meetings. That procedure produced the following agenda: 1) reunification of Germany, 2) European security, 3) disarmament, and 4) East-West contacts.[20]

The Geneva Conference of Heads of Government, as the summit was officially designated, convened on schedule (July 18) in the solemn and somewhat overbearing decor of the Palais des Nations, the former headquarters of the League of Nations. According to one estimate, the total number of attendees exceeded twelve hundred. Western principals, besides President Eisenhower and Secretary Dulles, included Prime Minister Eden and Foreign Secretary Harold Macmillan of Britain and Premier Faure and Foreign Minister Antoine Pinay of France. On the Soviet delegation, Premier Nikolai Bulganin was the nominal

---

[18]Address by President Eisenhower, "To Seek the Road to Peace," in U.S. Department of State, *Bulletin*, Vol. 33, No. 839 (July 25, 1955), p. 132.

[19]Eubank, in *Summit Conferences*, p. 142, states the following: "Within the Western camp all was disunity. Eden did not like the rigid timetable; there was too much rushing. He asked for preliminary meetings of the Western heads of government but Eisenhower refused. . . . Faure was concerned about security and disarmament; Eden wanted to press for German reunification. Eisenhower had another idea. He proposed to 'define the crucial world problems and then issue a directive to the foreign ministers to work out the details and conduct negotiations."

[20]U.S. Congress, House Committee on Foreign Affairs, 96th Congress, 1st Session, Special Study Series on Foreign Affairs Issues, Vol. I: *Soviet Diplomacy and Negotiating Behavior: Emerging New Context for U.S. Diplomacy*, prepared by the Senior Specialists Division, Congressional Research Service, Library of Congress (Washington: U.S. Government Printing Office, 1979), p. 312.

head, accompanied by Foreign Minister Molotov, Communist Party Secretary General Nikita Khrushchev, Deputy Foreign Minister Andrei Gromyko, and Defense Minister Marshal Georgi Zhukov. As the only chief of state present, Eisenhower acted as conference chairman and opened the proceedings by suggesting that the attention of the conferees center on German reunification through free elections, disarmament with inspection, and the peaceful and cooperative uses of atomic energy. Premier Faure stressed the need to end the Cold War and resolve the German problem, as did Prime Minister Macmillan. Premier Bulganin called for an end to the armaments race, a ban on nuclear testing, and limitations on the size of armed forces. Subsequent highlights of the discussions included Eisenhower's "Open Skies" proposal and Bulganin's 26-nation European Security Treaty to replace NATO and the Warsaw Pact, the latter having been formed earlier that spring (May 15) in response to West German independence and entry into NATO. But in one manner or another, the conference proceedings became marked by formalism and tedium,[21] resulting in what has been described as "a restatement of known mutually unacceptable positions."[22]

There were no formal agreements signed at the conference. The final communiqué of July 23 took the form of a directive to the foreign ministers to pursue negotiations on three issues: 1) European security and Germany, 2) disarmament, and 3) development of contacts between East and West.[23] In compliance, the foreign ministers met in Geneva from October 27 through November 16 that same year but achieved little, if anything. At those meetings,

---

[21]Ibid.
[22]Ibid., p. 314.
[23]U.S. Department of State, *Bulletin*, Vol. 33, No. 840 (August 1, 1955), pp. 176-77. (Text of the Directive to Foreign Ministers, July 23, 1955).

Dulles reported that Molotov rejected all of the Western proposals on German reunification and European security, in effect repudiating the communiqué and deadlocking the meetings. Eisenhower's return cable to Dulles stated: "... The clear breach of Summit directive creates a condition where no confidence can be placed on agreements with Soviet Government and ... we shall have to conduct our relations accordingly."[24] The meetings disbanded in failure.

Although Eisenhower never had any illusions about the prospects at Geneva, he did, in retrospect, evaluate the summit as a "limited success."[25] His "Open Skies" proposal won favorable world attention even though it was rejected almost out of hand by the Soviets. Bulganin initially showed interest in it, but Khrushchev shut the door on further progress because he considered it "a bald espionage plot against the U.S.S.R."[26] It was from this difference that Eisenhower concluded that Khrushchev held the real power in the Soviet delegation and not Bulganin, the nominal head.[27] The conference was also a success in the sense that Western unity held on the German reunification issue and on rejection of Soviet attempts to trade this off for a European security pact that would dissolve NATO and, in effect, break Western strength and cohesion in Europe.

That rejection notwithstanding, the Soviets also had

---

[24]Eisenhower, *Mandate for Change*, p. 529.

[25]Ibid., p. 530.

[26]Ibid., p. 521.

[27]Ibid.: "As was my custom, I mingled with the Soviet delegation. We walked together to the cocktail lounge. Daily, at adjournment time, we participated in what was apparently an international substitute for the British hour of tea. On this occasion, as it happened, I walked with Mr. Khrushchev. 'I don't agree with the chairman,' he said, smiling—but there was no smile in his voice. I saw clearly then, for the first time, the identity of the real boss of the Soviet delegation.

"From that moment until the final adjournment of the conference, I wasted no more time probing Mr. Bulganin; I devoted myself exclusively to an attempt to persuade Mr. Khrushchev of the merits of the Open Skies plan, but to no avail."

reason to view the summit as a partial success. As recounted by Khrushchev in his memoirs:

> We returned to Moscow from Geneva knowing that we hadn't achieved any concrete results. But we were encouraged, realizing now that our enemies probably feared us as much as we feared them.... The Geneva meeting was an important breakthrough for us on the diplomatic front. We had established ourselves as able to hold our own in the international arena.[28]

Khrushchev's State Visit and Camp David Meeting, September 15–27, 1959

UPON HIS RETURN to Moscow after the Geneva summit, Ambassador Bohlen found that the Soviet press made much of "the spirit of Geneva" and Soviet diplomats set out to capitalize upon their new-found international status.[29] Bulganin and Khrushchev embarked on an ambitious tour of Asia, the Middle East and Africa to project an enhanced image of communism to the world. But in Eastern Europe, the "spirit" helped to incite the Poznan riots in Poland early in 1956 and eventually led to the Hungarian revolt and its suppression in November of that year. The lesson of

---

[28]Nikita Khrushchev, *Khrushchev Remembers*, with Introduction, Commentary and Notes by Edward Crankshaw, trans. and ed. Strobe Talbott (Boston: Little, Brown & Co., 1970), p. 400. Also see, for example, Strobe Talbott's "Social Issues," Chapter 8 in *The Making of America's Soviet Policy*, ed. Joseph S. Nye, Jr. (New Haven: Yale University Press, 1984), pp. 194-95, wherein he states: "It was Nikita Khrushchev's coming-out. It gave him the self-confidence and the pretext for initiating some important, lasting changes once he got home. Within months, Khrushchev had delivered his Secret Speech launching the de-Stalinization campaign....

"Khrushchev probably would not have given the Secret Speech, nor would he have released so many prisoners from the Gulag, nor could he have defeated the so-called Anti-Party Group (which he accomplished with the decisive backing of Marshal Georgi Zhukov, the personification of the Soviet military-security complex) had it not been for the relaxation of East-West conflict after the Geneva summit of 1955."

[29]Bohlen, *Witness to History*, pp. 388-89.

Geneva became clear: to the Soviets, Western interest in peace translated to Western noninterference in Soviet control of the East European satellites. The Suez crisis brought about by Nasser's announcement of Egyptian nationalization of the canal in July 1956, followed by the short-lived Anglo-French-Israeli invasion, brought back the Cold War confrontation between Moscow and Washington that both had proclaimed they wanted to end in Geneva.

Behind the scenes, however, there developed a rather lengthy dialogue by correspondence between the two capitals about the need for another summit conference. On the heels of the dramatic launching of the Sputniks of October 4 and November 3, 1957, Premier Bulganin sent a fifteen-page letter to Eisenhower in December formally proposing an East-West summit conference to discuss arms control and an end to nuclear testing. The timing of his letter was obvious—a week before the Paris meeting of the North Atlantic Summit Conference at which the U.S. (as previously announced) would propose arming Western Europe with U.S. missiles and nuclear weapons. Eisenhower's reply of January 12, 1958 conditionally accepted Bulganin's proposal, contingent on adequate preparations by the foreign ministers. He also suggested that the peaceful uses of outer space be included as an agenda item.[30]

After Khrushchev superseded Bulganin as premier (formally, chairman of the Council of Ministers) on March 27, 1958, he promptly transmitted, on April 5, his own letter

---

[30]On February 26, 1958, Eisenhower wrote the following to Hazlett: "Now we come to the Summit Conference. If we and our allies can first agree on the positions we will take on the various subjects that will be discussed; if the Russians will agree to a preparatory conference at a lower level; and if they will promise to abide by the agreements made at the preparatory conference—then, and only then, I am willing to meet with them. If this procedure is followed, I think we can at least hope for some success; any thing else is bound to bring dismal failure." Quoted in Griffith, *Ike's Letters*, p. 201.

to Eisenhower proposing a summit.[31] Eisenhower's reply amplified his preconditions for such a meeting to include adequate preparations by the foreign ministers, an acceptable agenda agreed upon in advance, and a reasonable chance that the summit would be successful.[32] Soviet interest in a nuclear test ban was underscored by Khrushchev's unilateral suspension of testing on March 31 and was followed by U.S. suspension in August.

With the outbreak of the crises in Jordan and Lebanon in July 1958, which included the landing of U.S. marines in Lebanon, Khrushchev again called for a summit meeting. This time he proposed that the heads of government of the U.S., U.S.S.R., Britain, France, and India attend, as well as U.N. Secretary General Dag Hammarskjöld and representatives of the Arab nations. After several exchanges Eisenhower rejected the proposal, primarily on the grounds that the proper forum for such discussions was the United Nations and that Khrushchev "was arrogating to himself" the privilege of selecting the conference attendees.[33]

Khrushchev decided upon more aggressive tactics. On November 27, 1958 he reignited the Berlin crisis by announcing that the wartime agreements were at an end, that Western occupation of Berlin was unlawful, and that Berlin must become a demilitarized free city within six months or he would sign a separate peace treaty with East Germany (to preclude access to the city). Having generated the crisis, he now repeated his calls for a summit conference, but these were again rejected by Washington on the 10th of January, 1959. Instead, Eisenhower proposed a

---

[31]Plischke, *Summit Diplomacy*, p. 35. This was the twenty-seventh letter in the series of Soviet correspondence with President Eisenhower, according to Plischke.

[32]Ibid., p. 83.

[33]Dwight D. Eisenhower, *The White House Years: Waging Peace, 1956-1961* (Garden City: Doubleday & Co., 1965), p. 284.

meeting of the foreign ministers of the Four Powers with discussions to be limited to the subject at hand, Berlin and a German peace treaty. Eisenhower insisted that, although he was prepared to "go the extra mile," substantive progress by the foreign ministers was the prerequisite for a summit.[34] Early the next month, February, Dulles was sent abroad to meet with Macmillan, de Gaulle, and Adenauer to consolidate Western unity on the Berlin crisis.

Eisenhower reiterated his position in a television address on March 16, but was personally "amazed" the next day when his remark about the need for substantive progress by the foreign ministers was construed in the press as only a perfunctory requirement for a summit conference.[35] On March 20 and 21, President Eisenhower conferred with the British foreign minister at Camp David. Macmillan pushed for the summit; but in this regard he was somewhat out of step with Eisenhower and the other allies on the urgency of a summit. They did, however, come to agreement on the wording of a diplomatic note to the Soviet government that clarified Eisenhower's intentions about the foreign ministers' meeting and its relation to a summit:

> The purpose of the Foreign Minister[s'] meeting should be to reach positive agreements over as wide a field as possible, and in any case to narrow the differences between the respective points of view and to prepare

---

[34]Ibid., p. 346: "But the men in the Kremlin were all aware of our long-standing insistence that, while we would always go the extra mile to negotiate where there was any logical hope of progress, we would not, in its absence, go to a summit."

[35]Ibid., p. 350: "The next morning in reading the newspapers I was amazed to learn that my remarks of the evening before had been interpreted to mean that I agreed to a summit meeting as long as a foreign ministers' conference was held first.... Those who were anxious for a summit meeting took my words to mean that no matter what happened at the foreign ministers' meeting I would interpret it in such a way as to justify going ahead at the summit. That was exactly the opposite of what I sought to convey. I was determined to make the Soviets show ahead of time that there would be promise in a summit, before I would attend such a meeting."

constructive proposals for consideration by a conference of Heads of Government later in the summer. On
this understanding and as soon as developments in the
Foreign Minister[s'] meeting justify holding a Summit
Conference, the United States Government would be
ready to participate in such a conference. The date,
place and agenda for such a conference would be
proposed by the meeting of Foreign Ministers.[36]

Encouraged by the prospects for his long-sought summit,
Khrushchev agreed to the meeting of the ministers at the
end of the month, and the talks commenced in Geneva on
May 11, 1959. Secretary of State Christian Herter, who had
replaced Dulles only four days before the commencement
of the meeting due to Dulles' failing health, reported little
progress. The discussions plodded on for forty-one days
until they recessed on June 20. Eisenhower and Herter
suspected the Soviets of deliberately stalling. The president
wrote Khrushchev on the 15th of June to clarify yet again
the link between progress at the meeting and the convening
of a summit conference, countering Foreign Minister
Gromyko's statement in Geneva that no link existed.[37]
Macmillan, in contrast, was anxious for a summit without
any preconditions.

Pressure to break the impasse mounted in July when
First Deputy Premier Frol Kozlov visited the United States
for ten days in connection with a Soviet exhibition in New
York. His U.S. host, Vice President Nixon, was, in turn,
invited to visit Moscow with the U.S. trade exhibition later
in the year (an event that prompted his meeting and
famous "kitchen debate" with Khrushchev), and Kozlov
began dropping hints of other high-level visits. Following
an uneventful meeting between Kozlov and Eisenhower in

---

[36]Ibid., Appendix S, "Note," p. 697.

[37]Ibid., p. 400. Eisenhower wrote: "Mr. Gromyko has stated that 'in the opinion
of the Soviet Government there is no foundation for any link between the results
of this (Geneva Foreign Ministers') conference and the convening of a summit
meeting'. . . . " This was clearly unacceptable to Eisenhower.

Washington, the president was asked about a report from Moscow that Khrushchev was letting it be known he was interested in coming to the United States for a visit himself. Eisenhower deferred comment, stating that he hadn't heard of that report. But apparently the idea began to grow on him; as Kozlov prepared to depart on July 12, Under Secretary of State Robert Murphy conveyed a personal invitation from the president for Khrushchev to visit for informal talks.

But apparently there was some confusion between the president and the under secretary about the conditions under which the invitation was offered. In short order, Khrushchev accepted the invitation. However, the president noted the absence of any reference to the subject of progress by the foreign ministers in Geneva. A subsequent discussion with Under Secretary Murphy soon disclosed that no preconditions for the Khrushchev invitation had been conveyed to Kozlov, as Eisenhower had assumed. Murphy stated that it was not his understanding that the link should have been made and the invitation had been delivered unqualified. As recalled by Eisenhower in his memoirs:

> To say that this news disturbed me is an understate-
> ment. My invitation was to a meeting that I had
> described as a prelude to a summit; since my readiness
> to attend a summit was conditioned on assurance of
> progress at Geneva, it was difficult for me to understand
> how the misinterpretation occurred.... The residual
> effects of all this caused me some chagrin: I now had to
> meet Khrushchev and allow him to tour our country in
> spite of the fact that he had deliberately engineered the
> breakdown of the foreign ministers' meeting.[38]

Now stuck, a less-than-enthusiastic president announced Khrushchev's visit on August 5 and later in the month

---

[38]Ibid., pp. 407 and 412.

headed for Europe for consultations with the allies. Meeting in Bonn with West German President Theodor Heuss and Chancellor Adenauer, Eisenhower agreed to remain firm on Berlin and support the buildup of German armed forces for NATO. The chancellor also voiced his opinion that the prospects for improved East-West contacts, as previously discussed at the Geneva summit, remained pessimistic. Following a visit with the British royal family at Balmoral Castle, Eisenhower met at Chequers with Prime Minister Macmillan. They agreed that the most important objective was to get Khrushchev to accept a moratorium on the threats and counterthreats regarding West Berlin. In subsequent talks with the prime minister, an agenda was proposed that included nuclear test bans, disarmament, and better East-West contacts. Later in Paris, President de Gaulle conveyed his impression of the futility of talks with Khrushchev without some tangible evidence of progress in advance of a summit and suggested that Eisenhower stand resolute on the Berlin situation.

In his last week before Khrushchev's arrival, Eisenhower settled on three objectives for the talks: 1) to convey clearly the U.S. stand on Berlin and firmness on U.S. rights elsewhere; 2) to convince Khrushchev that he was willing to go to a summit but not under Soviet threats or where no prospect of success was indicated; and 3) to focus on the Soviet leader's personal opportunity to become a great statesman if he used his power to further the prospects for peace, disarmament and relaxation of tensions.[39] On the last point, Eisenhower remarked to legislators that he wanted to make "one great personal effort, before leaving office, to soften up the Soviet leader" and that, except for the Austrian State Treaty, "we haven't made a chip in the granite in seven years."[40]

---

[39]Ibid., p. 432.
[40]Ibid.

Upon Khrushchev's arrival on September 15, the two leaders met in the Oval Office for two hours and agreed that the foreign ministers should attend to the agenda while the Soviet leader was on his tour of the country. Khrushchev said his main objective for the talks was to establish a trust between them based upon acceptance of each other's existence, and he extended an invitation to Eisenhower for a return visit to Moscow. Secretary Herter and Foreign Minster Gromyko met for forty-five minutes the next morning, September 16, and reached preliminary agreement on the order of the subjects to be discussed. Other U.S. participants included Deputy Under Secretary of State Livingston Merchant, Deputy Assistant Secretary for European Affairs Foy Kohler, and Richard Davis, Counselor at the American Embassy in Moscow.[41]

Under escort by Henry Cabot Lodge, U.S. ambassador to the U.N., Khrushchev's tour included New York, Los Angeles, San Francisco, Des Moines and Ames, Iowa, Pittsburgh, and then Camp David for the final weekend of discussions.[42]

At Camp David, Khrushchev was joined by Foreign Minister Gromyko, Ambassador Mikhail Menshikov, and A.A. Soldatov, chief of the American Department in the Ministry of Foreign Affairs, among others. Vice President Nixon, Secretary Herter, and Ambassador Lodge joined in with other officials on the American side.

In their discussions, Khrushchev pushed hard to get Eisenhower to commit himself to a four-power summit; but the president responded that he would never agree to that under "the faintest semblance of an ultimatum" regarding Soviet threats of signing a separate treaty with East

---

[41]U.S. Department of State, *Bulletin*, Vol. 41, No. 1058 (October 5, 1959), p. 479.

[42]The Camp David meetings took place from September 25th to September 27th.

Germany. As recounted by Eisenhower, the agenda was "practically ignored." Their talks proceeded "somewhat haphazardly," but kept coming back "to Berlin and the latest Soviet ultimatum."[43]

The standoff continued until the last day of the talks, when Khrushchev finally agreed to lift his ultimatum in exchange for Eisenhower's acceptance of a summit. However, he could not do so publicly, he said, at least not in the final communiqué of the conference. Eisenhower stated that unless the Soviet leader made public his rescission, there would be no agreement. A compromise was then struck: Eisenhower would wait a few days after the conference, then announce that the Soviets agreed to lift their time limit on Berlin and that he had therefore agreed to visit Moscow and attend a summit. The delay would enable Khrushchev to explain matters once in Moscow, and he would then confirm the accuracy of Eisenhower's announcement.

The face-saving construct was subsequently carried out as planned. The communiqué of September 27 simply stated that negotiations on Berlin would be reopened subject to the approval of the other parties concerned, reaffirmed agreement on the importance of disarmament, and announced that the president's return visit would be arranged through diplomatic channels.[44]

---

[43]Eisenhower, *Waging Peace*, p. 444. Eisenhower further observed: "During the sessions the Chairman and I seized several opportunities for strictly private conversations, some at Camp David, others while sight-seeing around the countryside. Because my purpose in these man-to-man talks was to learn about his intentions, objectives, and personal characteristics, we used a single interpreter only—his own."

[44]The Joint Communiqué, released September 27, 1959, stated this as follows: "With respect to the specific Berlin question, an understanding was reached, subject to the approval of the other parties directly concerned, that negotiations would be reopened with a view to achieving a solution which would be in accordance with the interests of all concerned and in the interest of international peace." The complete text is reproduced in U.S. Department of State, *Bulletin*, Vol. 41, No. 1059 (October 12, 1959), p. 499, and appears with other such documents on each summit in the Appendix to this study.

Khrushchev took great pride in his American visit and claimed it was a "colossal moral victory" despite the fact that the talks had been generally unproductive.[45] He saw the visit as an explicit recognition of Moscow's strength and international status and, for reasons not apparent in the West at the time, made much of this in a follow-on trip to China from September 30 through October 4.

The Paris Heads of Government Conference, May 16–17, 1960

K HRUSCHEV HAILED HIS visit to the United States as a great personal triumph and a victory for the Soviet Union. His memoirs are replete with references to "the spirit of Camp David," a phrase that Eisenhower never deemed valid. To Khrushchev it meant recognition of a relationship between Moscow and Washington based more on equality than in the past. The following is representative:

> ... [T]he reason we were proud was that we had finally forced the United States to recognize the necessity of establishing closer contacts with us. If the President of the United States himself invites the Chairman of the Council of Ministers of the USSR, then you know conditions have changed. We'd come a long way from the time when the United States wouldn't even grant us diplomatic recognition. We felt pride in our country, our Party, our people, and the victories they had achieved.[46]

---

[45]Nikita Khrushchev, *Khrushchev Remembers: The Last Testament*, trans. and ed. Strobe Talbott (Boston: Little, Brown & Co., 1974), p. 415: "Even if we didn't reap material benefits right away, my talks with Eisenhower represented a colossal moral victory.... Most important: the Americans took the initiative of inviting us to their country after a long ideological war. They had no hope—and they certainly didn't succeed—in forcing us to compromise our basic principles and dignity. On the contrary, we emerged from the visit and the talks with our position in the world strengthened, firm as a rock, and ready to defend our positions in the future."

[46]Ibid., p. 374.

A discernible thaw followed Camp David, highlighted by the simmering down of the Berlin situation, a U.S.-Soviet cultural exchange agreement on November 21, 1959, and the Antarctic Treaty of December 1. But the thaw was fleeting. On January 14, 1960, in a speech before the Supreme Soviet, Khrushchev began to renew his threat to sign a separate peace with East Germany. He then orchestrated an announcement of February 4 that the Warsaw Pact countries were also committed to that course of action.

Meanwhile, the Western heads of state and government had met in Paris and Rambouillet from December 19–21 for an exchange of views on various subjects, including Berlin and plans for the summit meeting that Eisenhower had agreed to at Camp David. The final communiqué stated that the Western allies were in accord on the desirability of a meeting with Khrushchev, proposed a date of April 27, 1960, and suggested Paris for its location. In the discussions, Prime Minister Macmillan advocated that the Western powers seek an interim agreement with Khrushchev whereby limited concessions would be offered in exchange for Soviet guarantees of unrestricted Western rights of access to Berlin. Chancellor Adenauer staunchly rejected that proposal and stated that he would oppose any interim agreement that would attempt to alter the status of Western powers in Germany. President de Gaulle, while firm on Berlin, opposed Eisenhower's proposals for a closer integration of NATO forces. There was no general agreement among the four leaders on how to respond to Khrushchev's previous proposals on disarmament.

In the end, however, they agreed the meeting would be useful and established procedures to follow in preparation for it. Invitations were sent to Khrushchev on December 21 by Eisenhower, de Gaulle and Macmillan and were accepted by the Soviet leader. (A subsequent exchange changed the convening date to May 16, 1960, due to a conflict in Khrushchev's schedule.) Immediately following the Heads of State and Government meeting, on December 22, the Ministerial Meeting of the North Atlantic Council issued a communiqué reaffirming Western solidarity on the Berlin situation and emphasized "once again that the Alliance must remain vigilant and strong."[47]

President de Gaulle had wanted Khrushchev to visit Paris in advance of the summit, and he did so from March 23 through April 2. While there, Khrushchev affirmed his intentions of signing a separate treaty with East Germany, but was confronted with de Gaulle's equally firm show of Western solidarity against any such move. Later in the month, on April 25, Khrushchev's threats became more ominous in a blistering speech he delivered at Baku, capital of the Azerbaijan S.S.R. Following this, a NATO Council convened on May 2–4 in Istanbul for consultations and once again reaffirmed Western solidarity on Berlin. But other events were also taking place at the time in Turkey.

Unrelated to the Council meeting, a United States U-2 reconnaissance plane had taken off from its base in eastern Turkey on the previous day, May 1, and commenced a scheduled mission over the Soviet Union. It was to be the last mission for pilot Francis Gary Powers, however, for the high-flying aircraft was brought down by Soviet missiles near Sverdlovsk later in the day. On May 3, NASA, as the cover agency for U-2 flights, announced that one of its "weather reconnaissance planes" was missing. Two days later, on May 5, it was announced in Moscow that the plane had been shot down while on a spy mission deep inside Soviet territory. Assuming that the plane had been destroyed and its pilot killed, the State Department put out a cover story that only worsened the U.S. posture in what was

---

[47]U.S. Department of State, *Bulletin*, Vol. 42, No. 1072 (January 11, 1960), p. 45. The North Atlantic Council's previous statement of principles on Berlin was issued on December 16, 1958.

soon to be revealed as a clever trap being baited by Khrushchev.

After the cover story was made public, stating that the weather plane may have strayed inadvertently into Soviet air space, Khrushchev sprang his trap—he announced that pilot Powers had been taken alive and was in his custody. Faced with this irrefutable evidence, Eisenhower was finally forced to admit to the true nature of the aircraft and its mission. On May 7 he publicly announced this and said he had authorized such flights as a means to ensure against surprise attack from the Soviet Union. He took full responsibility for the incident and declared that further flights had been suspended.

A week later, Khrushchev and Defense Minister Rodion Malinovsky arrived in Paris two days before the scheduled opening of the summit conference. Khrushchev immediately presented President de Gaulle, the conference host, with a list of demands that Eisenhower would have to meet before Khrushchev would be willing to attend the summit. His demands were that Eisenhower publicly apologize for espionage flights, renounce their continuance, and "pass severe judgement" on those responsible. Upon Eisenhower's arrival de Gaulle informed him of the demands, whereupon Eisenhower said he would not foreswear future reconnaissance efforts by the United States and that he had already informed Khrushchev by separate communication that he would not apologize for the flight.

At the opening session of the conference at the Elysée Palace on May 16, President de Gaulle called the meeting to order and was about to let Eisenhower, as the senior statesman present, commence his opening address, when a highly agitated demand to speak came from Khrushchev. De Gaulle demurred, but with a consenting nod from Eisenhower, allowed the Soviet leader to speak first. Khrushchev then undertook a twenty-minute harangue

against the United States in which he reiterated his
demands and announced that Eisenhower's invitation to
visit the Soviet Union had been revoked. He then stormed
out of the Palace, leaving the three Western leaders to
ponder their next move. They thereupon decided to
reschedule the proceedings to late afternoon on May 17th
and inquired if Khrushchev planned to attend. The reply,
asked for and delivered in writing, was negative: he
would not meet unless his demands were met. After
delivering another tirade at a news conference on the 18th,
Khrushchev departed. A tripartite communiqué was issued
by the Western leaders simply stating that they regretted
Khrushchev's attitude and would remain ready to negotiate
at a suitable time in the future.[48]

The collapse of the summit triggered further strains in
East-West relations. The Soviets broke off their participation in U.N. disarmament talks on June 27. Several days
later, on July 1, they shot down an unarmed U.S. RB-47
reconnaissance plane over international waters in the
Barents Sea. Khrushchev's increasing belligerence was
displayed in his "shoe-banging" incident at the United
Nations the following September. His anger was due not so
much to the collapse of the summit for which he had
labored so long, nor even to the U-2 incident, but rather to
his own inability to make good on his threats in the face of
Western resolve on Berlin.

It is speculative as to whether Khrushchev deliberately
scuttled the Paris summit and seized upon the U-2 incident
as a plausible excuse under orders from Moscow, or
whether his plans changed en route. In his memoirs,
Khrushchev makes the latter case:

> We were haunted by the fact that just prior to this
> meeting the United States had dared to send its U-2
> reconnaissance plane against us. It was as though the

---

[48]Department of State, *Bulletin* Vol. 42, No. 1093 (June 6, 1960), pp. 905-6.

Americans had deliberately tried to place a time bomb under the meeting, set to go off just as we were about to sit down with them at the negotiating table. What else could we expect from such a country? Could we really expect it to come to a reasonable agreement with us? No! So the conference was doomed before it began.... Our reputation depended on our making some sort of protest: we owed it to world public opinion, particularly public opinion in Communist countries.... Thus we left Moscow with a set of documents pointing in one direction, and we landed in Paris with documents pointing in the opposite direction.[49]

However that may be, Eisenhower judged that Khrushchev's brief attempt at a more conciliatory policy with the West—"the Camp David spirit"—was seen in Moscow as a failure because of Khrushchev's inability to split the allies on the Berlin issue. After the collapse of the Paris summit, the Cold War resumed and intensified. "The peaceful line was gone," observed Eisenhower, and "in its place was a Kremlin attitude reminiscent of the days of Stalin."[50]

The wisdom of scheduling the U-2 flight so close to the summit conference has been questioned sufficiently by others in the ensuing record, but several points should be made clear before leaving the incident to the history books. First, the flights commenced in 1956, a year after the Geneva summit at which Eisenhower had made an earnest attempt to institute reciprocal reconnaissance through his "Open Skies" proposal. Adequate inspection guarantees have been a U.S. prerequisite ever since for serious discussion of arms control measures with the Soviets. At the time, however, the reconnaissance flights were not tied to arms control, but were intended, rather, to protect against the possibilities of a Soviet surprise attack; and an accurate assessment of that depended on good intelligence.

---

[49]Khrushchev, *The Last Testament*, pp. 450-52.
[50]Eisenhower, *Waging Peace*, p. 560.

In that regard, the following evaluation was made by Eisenhower:

> During the four years of its operations, the U-2 program produced intelligence of critical importance to the United States. Perhaps as important as the positive information—what the Soviets did have—was the negative information it produced—what the Soviets did not have. Intelligence gained from this source produced proof that the horrors of the alleged "bomber gap" and the later "missile gap" were nothing more than imaginative creations of irresponsibility.[51]

Further, Khrushchev's account of his indignation over the May 1960 U-2 flight and how it caused the summit to collapse appears misplaced, since U.S. intelligence knew from the start of the operations in 1956 that the Soviets were well aware of the missions—they were just not able to shoot the planes down due to their high altitude. So rather than protest the flights earlier, which would, in effect, show an embarrassing weakness on their part, the Soviets simply kept quiet until their capabilities were sufficiently improved. Thus, Khrushchev's rage, if real, was more likely based on the frustration of several years than on sudden indignation just before the start of the summit.

By one measure or another, the rift between Moscow and Washington was widening again, and relations were too strained to encourage any movement toward further negotiations between East and West. The legacy of the Paris summit is that it was the last attempt to approach summits on an East-West basis: the eight summits that followed were bilateral meetings between the U.S. and the Soviets. Although the British and French have had separate summits with the Soviet leaders, Paris 1960 marked the end of combined allied efforts at summit conferences with the Soviets.

---

[51]Ibid., p. 547.

3

The Vienna and Glassboro Summit Meetings

Kennedy and Khrushchev at Vienna, June 3–4, 1961

KHRUSHCHEV'S INVECTIVE AGAINST Eisenhower at the aborted Paris summit made the prospects for future diplomacy at that level more problematic, but the opportunity arose sooner than either side had reason to expect with the election of John F. Kennedy. At the Kennedy-Khrushchev meeting in Vienna in June 1961, the Soviet leader continued to vent his anger and frustration on his less experienced counterpart and renewed his threats on Berlin in stark terms. The discussions were frank and even brutal at times, as Khrushchev pulled out the stops and took every advantage he could of the young president. He desperately needed to score a victory on the Soviet homefront on the lingering German problem.[1]

---

[1] W.W. Rostow, *The Diffusion of Power* (New York: The Macmillan Co., 1972), p. 223: "Khrushchev's inclination to probe further at the West was almost certainly reinforced by his political situation at home, notably weakened since the U-2 incident and the breakup of the Paris summit meeting. He badly needed a success in foreign policy to strengthen his hand within the Presidium."

Earlier in the year, Deputy Special Assistant for National Security Affairs Walt W. Rostow, in his first memorandum to the new president on January 21, 1961, drew up a list of seventeen questions related to U.S.-Soviet affairs, including prospects for a summit meeting with Khrushchev, and forwarded it to the president. Later, on February 11, President Kennedy conducted a lengthy review of U.S. relations with the Soviets with Secretary of State Dean Rusk, Special Assistant for National Security Affairs McGeorge Bundy, and four experts who had served as ambassadors to Moscow (the incumbent ambassador, Llewellyn Thompson, and former ambassadors Charles Bohlen, George Kennan, and Averell Harriman).[2] At this meeting Kennedy stated that a personal, informal meeting with Khrushchev might be useful but that " . . . a summit is not a place to carry on negotiations which involve details."[3] Beyond the specific substantive issues on which some progress might be expected, such as a cease-fire in Laos and a nuclear test ban agreement,

> . . . the President was attracted by the meeting as offering an opportunity to define the framework for future American-Soviet relations. Kennedy saw the world as in a state of uncontrollable change, rushing in directions no one could foresee. . . . [A]nd the overriding need, he felt, was to prevent direct confrontations between Russian and American power in the chaotic time ahead. He intended to propose, in effect, a standstill in the cold war so that neither great nuclear state, in the inevitable competition around the planet, would find itself committed to actions which would risk its essential security, threaten the existing balance of force or endanger world peace.[4]

---

[2]Theodore C. Sorensen, *Kennedy* (New York: Harper & Row, 1965), pp. 541-42.
[3]Ibid., p. 542.
[4]Arthur M. Schlesinger, Jr., *A Thousand Days: John F. Kennedy in the White House* (Boston: Houghton Mifflin, 1965), p. 348.

Discussions in the diplomatic channel, followed by private letter exchanges, resulted in Khrushchev's agreement on March 9 to meet in Vienna on June 3 and 4. Khrushchev's memoirs state that the proposals from Washington suggested a "neutral" location for the meeting and that Helsinki, Geneva and Vienna were considered.[5]

In preparation, Rostow sent Kennedy another memorandum on March 26, "SUBJECT: Medium-Level Conversation with Mr. Khrushchev," in which he considered several troublesome areas in U.S.-Soviet relations: Cuba, Laos, and particularly the Viet Cong offensive in the Mekong Delta. His conclusion was as follows: "What we need to get through this period without war is a most serious understanding between the U.S. and the Soviet Union about the limits within which force shall be used."[6]

Kennedy agreed that the level of talks should be geared to the relation between power and ideology, with the objective of coming to agreement on how the two countries could avoid actions that threatened the peace between them. But, as the talks would later show, the leaders would approach that objective from different directions and be at cross-purposes. Kennedy was seeking to maintain the status quo by avoiding conflicts in areas where neither country had vital national interests. On the other hand, Khrushchev sought to promote national liberation movements without Western interference in areas undergoing change. The stage was already set for contradictions at the summit.

The White House announcement on May 19 of the president's impending European trip and meeting with Khrushchev stated that their talks were not for the purpose of negotiation or reaching agreement on major inter-

---

[5]Khrushchev, *The Last Testament*, p. 492.
[6]Rostow, *The Diffusion of Power*, p. 658, note 3.

national problems, but rather for a general exchange of views on major issues.[7] The president's standing, however, had just been dealt a severe setback with the Bay of Pigs disaster of April 17. Few believed that the summit with Khrushchev would accomplish much with that as the immediate background of the meeting.

The president's itinerary included a prior stop in Paris for consultations with President de Gaulle from May 31 through June 2. Based upon these discussions and his earlier preparations, he had three specific objectives in mind before arriving in Vienna on June 3rd: 1) to establish a rational basis for accommodation with the Soviets, 2) to introduce precision into each other's assessments, and 3) thereby to avoid miscalculations that might lead to confrontations between the two.[8] As recounted later by Rostow, "The problem, as Kennedy put it before lunch on June 3, was: how the two countries could avoid actions which would endanger peace under circumstances where they engaged in ideological competition. . . ."[9] As Kennedy sought to pursue his purposes, Khrushchev propounded his own conception of peaceful change in the world through wars of national liberation. On balance, neither made a meaningful impact on the other's position. Peaceful coexistence meant different things.

Despite that fundamental contradiction, however, Kennedy and Khrushchev did come to terms on the worsening situation in Laos. The two "agreed that what was at stake in Laos was not worth the risk of a superpower confrontation."[10] As stated in the joint communiqué of June 4:

---

[7]U.S. Department of State, *Bulletin*, Vol. 44, No. 1145 (June 5, 1961), p. 848.

[8]House Committee on Foreign Affairs, *Soviet Diplomacy*, p. 328.

[9]Rostow, *The Diffusion of Power*, pp. 224-25.

[10]Alexander L. George, "Political Crises," Chapter 6 in Nye, *America's Soviet Policy*, p. 139. In an earlier work George had observed: "The two sides recognized that achievement of the objective would require cooperation by other states, and they agreed to act in order to ensure the compliance of members of their political blocs. Eventually, in July 1962, a cease-fire was established, and fourteen nations

> The President and the Chairman reaffirmed their
> support of a neutral and independent Laos under a
> government chosen by the Laotians themselves, and of
> international agreements for insuring that neutrality
> and independence, and in this connection they have
> recognized the importance of an effective cease-fire.[11]

No progress was made toward an agreement on a ban of
nuclear testing, a subject that had been deadlocked in
Geneva prior to the summit. And neither Kennedy nor
Khrushchev changed established positions on Berlin and
Germany. Khrushchev renewed his threats about signing a
separate treaty with East Germany, a challenge that he
backed up with an aide-mémoire to Kennedy. If the United
States tried to maintain its position in Berlin after signature
of the treaty, warned Khrushchev, it would constitute a
violation of East German sovereignty and would be met
with force. Kennedy retorted, "It will be a cold winter."[12]
Khrushchev didn't wait for the snow to fall; in August the
Soviets resumed atmospheric nuclear testing and began
construction of the Berlin Wall.

Khrushchev acknowledged in his memoirs that despite
their differences, he was impressed with Kennedy at the
summit meeting: "He felt perfectly confident to answer
questions and make points on his own. This was to his
credit, and he rose in my estimation at once. He was, so to
speak, both my partner and my adversary."[13] But Arkady
Shevchenko, in *Breaking with Moscow*, presented a different
account:

---

signed the Declaration on the Neutrality of Laos. Although these arrangements
were short-lived, they did enable Kennedy to achieve his overriding objective of
conducting 'an honorable retreat from a strategically weak position.'" *Managing
U.S.-Soviet Rivalry: Problems of Crisis Intervention* (Boulder: Westview Press, 1963),
pp. 4-5.
    [11]U.S. Department of State, *Bulletin*, Vol. 44, No. 1148 (June 26, 1961), p. 999.
    [12]Roger Hilsman, *To Move a Nation* (Garden City: Doubleday & Co., 1967), p.
136.
    [13]Khrushchev, *The Last Testament*, pp. 497-98.

After the Vienna summit, Khrushchev concluded that
Kennedy would accept almost anything to avoid nuclear war. The lack of confidence the President displayed during the both Bay of Pigs invasion and the
Berlin crisis further confirmed this view....
[Khrushchev lectured] about Kennedy's "wishy-washy"
behavior, ending with the remark: "I know for certain
that Kennedy doesn't have a strong backbone, nor,
generally speaking, does he have the courage to stand
up to a serious challenge." Khrushchev's impression of
Kennedy was a prevalent one among Soviet leaders
generally.[14]

Johnson and Kosygin at Glassboro, June 23–25, 1967

IN THE WAKE OF the Cuban missile crisis, President
Kennedy's assassination, and Khrushchev's downfall,
the years after the Vienna summit produced little inclination and opportunity for either the U.S. or the Soviet Union
to pursue more discussions at the summit. The United
States had become more and more drawn into the Vietnam
quagmire, which became an obsession for President
Lyndon Baines Johnson, as indeed it had for the country as
a whole. Nonetheless, negotiations had achieved a basic
agreement with the Soviets on nuclear nonproliferation by
the end of 1966, and the Outer Space Treaty was signed
shortly thereafter on January 27, 1967. Both measures
added to the record of earlier progress on arms control
efforts, beginning in 1963 with the signing of the "Hot Line"
agreement and the Partial Nuclear Test Ban Treaty, and
carried forward by the ongoing Geneva Eighteen-Nation
Disarmament Commission.[15]

---

[14]Arkady N. Shevchenko, *Breaking with Moscow* (New York: Alfred A. Knopf,
1985), p. 117.
[15]Agreement on the "hot-line" teletype link was signed in Geneva on June 20,
1963, and it became operational on August 30 of that year. The Treaty Banning
Nuclear Weapons Tests in the Atmosphere, in Outer Space, and Under Water was
signed in Moscow on August 5, 1963.

Despite U.S. preoccupation with the Vietnam war, the president was becoming increasingly concerned about the dangers of nuclear weapons proliferation and the nuclear armaments race. The construction of a Soviet anti-ballistic missile (ABM) defense system around Moscow set off new concerns. The president conveyed these to Kosygin in a letter of January 21, 1967 suggesting that "it may prove desirable to have our highest authorities meet in Geneva or other mutually agreeable place to carry the matter forward."[16] U.S. Ambassador to Moscow Llewellyn Thompson was instructed to make an initial exploration of Soviet interest.

Some five weeks later, on February 27, Premier Kosygin replied by letter that he was "prepared to continue the exchange on questions relating to strategic rocket–nuclear weapons." He added that he would provide Ambassador Thompson with his thoughts on the matter and suggested that future talks between appropriate officials might focus on "the entire problem."[17] Despite this encouragement, however, no commitments were made as to where and when such talks should begin, possibly because there was some internal disagreement in Moscow as to how they could best proceed on the matter.

President Johnson wrote again on May 19 to reaffirm his interest in bilateral discussions on anti-ballistic missile systems, intercontinental ballistic missiles, and the need for agreement on nonproliferation. But before a reply was received, a new Middle East crisis intervened, the "Six-Day War" of June 1967, and prompted the Fifth Emergency Session of the United Nations General Assembly. Premier Alexei Kosygin's planned attendance provided an opportunity for impromptu talks with President Johnson.

---

[16]Lyndon Baines Johnson, *The Vantage Point: Perspectives of the Presidency 1963-1969* (New York: Holt, Rinehart and Winston, 1971), p. 480.
[17]Ibid.

As soon as it was learned that Kosygin planned to come to New York for the Emergency Session, pressures began to mount to use the occasion for bilateral talks as well. According to the Shevchenko account, Premier Kosygin was also under pressure from the Politburo to seek a meeting with President Johnson, but, in view of limited prospects for achieving productive results, was less than enthusiastic about it.[18] But then a somewhat anomalous situation developed upon his arrival.

President Johnson invited the premier to meet with him in Washington, but Kosygin refused and suggested they meet in New York. That proposal was not acceptable to the president and he, in turn, proposed they meet somewhere halfway between the cities, such as Maguire Air Force Base in New Jersey. Kosygin apparently felt that a meeting on a U.S. military installation would convey the wrong impression and be misunderstood and misinterpreted by his allies, and he refused. The delaying tactics and standoff continued until, almost out of desperation, New Jersey Governor Richard J. Hughes was called in to recommend a suitable site in his state that was midway between New York and Washington. His suggestion was that they meet at Glassboro State College. On June 22, less than twenty-four hours before their talks were to commence, the two leaders finally agreed on that location.

---

[18]Shevchenko, *Breaking with Moscow*, pp. 136-37, states the following: "In the summer of 1967 ... Kosygin was the Soviet leader charged with opening a dialogue with a U.S. President.... But he had practically no authority to make any commitments and was given very little room for flexibility, and Kosygin correctly anticipated that his meeting with Johnson would produce no progress on either issue. The prospect of returning to Moscow completely empty-handed disturbed him.... Failure in the discussions would undermine his prestige as a negotiator and would bolster Brezhnev's efforts to reduce Kosygin's role in foreign affairs. Yet the conference had to take place; it was a Politburo decision. For a short while, Kosygin thought he had found a way to avoid the meeting in an apparent impasse between the Politburo's instructions that he was on no account to travel to Washington and the Americans' refusal to have the President come to New York."

In his memoirs, President Johnson recalled the frantic last-minute preparations that ensued. Harried members of the advance team descended upon "Hollybush," the residence of the Glassboro College president, at eleven o'clock that night to set up appropriate security measures and install a massive communications network (all of which necessitated a certain rearrangement of an otherwise orderly residential lifestyle suited to a small college environment). After the team worked through the night, President Johnson arrived at 11:00 a.m., observing later that "preparations that ordinarily would have required twelve days or more had taken just twelve hours."[19] He was accompanied by Secretary of State Dean Rusk and Secretary of Defense Robert S. McNamara. Premier Kosygin, Foreign Minister Gromyko, and Ambassador Dobrynin arrived about two hours later, and the talks began.

The Soviet premier wanted to focus on the Middle East crisis and was adamant on a prompt withdrawal of Israeli forces from Egypt, almost to the point of threatening war over it, according to President Johnson.[20] He also insisted on a halt in U.S. bombing of North Vietnam and withdrawal of U.S. combat forces from the hostilities. The president, however, wanted to use the occasion to make some progress on concluding the nonproliferation agreement that was then deadlocked in negotiations in Geneva, as well as to convince Kosygin that the Moscow ABM system presented deepening concerns to Washington. He made some headway in the former by showing the Soviet leader that they were basically in agreement on the first two articles of the proposed treaty (but not on the third article, which contained the controversial safeguard provisions). This was reflected two weeks later in Geneva when the two sides did accept those portions of the treaty.

---

[19]Johnson, *Vantage Point*, p. 483.
[20]Ibid., p. 484.

But on the ABM system, little progress was made despite Secretary McNamara's attempt to explain the interrelation between that system and offensive missiles, an explanation that Kosygin listened to with some disbelief. McNamara's argument was grounded in the concept of "mutual assured destruction." He explained to Kosygin that a defensive arms race would only exacerbate the existing offensive arms race[21] and thus destabilize the delicate balance between the two superpowers based on nuclear deterrence.[22] Kosygin appeared somewhat astonished by the presentation. The Soviet position was that defensive missile systems, such as the "Galosh" ABM system around Moscow, were built to save lives and, therefore, instead of discussing their limitation, the problem of offensive strategic weapons should be dealt with first.[23]

Although it is likely that Kosygin had no authority from the Politburo to negotiate on such matters at the time, possibly because Moscow wanted to attain nuclear parity with the United States before considering what limitations should apply, the discussions on that subject did initiate the strategic arms limitation talks in 1969 that eventually achieved fruition in the ABM Treaty of 1972.

On balance, however, there was not much to show in evidence of a productive summit meeting.[24] No agreements

---

[21]Strobe Talbott, *Deadly Gambits: The Reagan Administration and the Stalemate in Nuclear Arms Control* (New York: Alfred A. Knopf, 1984), p. 211.

[22]See also Rostow, *The Diffusion of Power*, pp. 384-90.

[23]Shevchenko, *Breaking with Moscow*, p. 201.

[24]It might be observed here that Premier Kosygin's title—chairman of the Council of Ministers of the Soviet Union—is equal, by protocol, to that of head of government. President Podgorny, as chairman of the Presidium of the Supreme Soviet, would have been, technically, the chief of state at the time. But Brezhnev held the real political power as secretary of the CPSU and was consolidating his control. As observed by Shevchenko (see note 18 above), the Politburo had given Kosygin little or no authority to make commitments during his meeting with President Johnson, and this may explain the unproductive results to some degree. Glassboro was the only one of the ten postwar summits not attended by the party secretary.

were signed and no joint communiqués were issued. For a short time, there was some talk of "the spirit of Hollybush" and both the president and Secretary Rusk said that the "hard-working" talks were highly useful. Premier Kosygin was later reported to have said simply, "We agreed on next to nothing."[25]

President Johnson made good on his efforts to stem the proliferation of nuclear weapons when the Non-Proliferation Treaty was signed by the U.S., the U.S.S.R., the U.K., and 59 other countries on July 1, 1968. A month later the text of an announcement was being readied for release stating that he would be visiting Leningrad and Moscow in the fall, but that was cancelled due to the Soviet invasion of Czechoslovakia in mid-August. Just before Christmas Johnson made one last attempt to meet with Kosygin again, through a proposal that Ambassador Thompson conveyed to Moscow; but this was declined by the Soviet leader, who preferred instead to await the forthcoming change in administrations.

[25]Shevchenko, *Breaking with Moscow*, p. 137.

4

The Nixon-Brezhnev Summits

In terms of their sheer complexity and scope, the three Nixon-Brezhnev summit meetings vastly exceeded the previous five encounters between U.S. and Soviet leaders in the postwar years and produced a host of agreements, the most notable of which embodied accords on strategic arms limitations for the first time in the history of the strained relations between the two countries. The interrelationship between these summits and developments in strategic weapons, the war in Vietnam, and the onset of a period of détente has been addressed in copious volumes and intense debates ever since. For the far more limited purposes of this study, only the main currents of these events will be addressed as they relate to the circumstances and motivations leading to the summit.

The Moscow Summit, May 22–30, 1972

PRESIDENT RICHARD M. NIXON had campaigned on the promise of ending U.S. involvement in the Vietnam war. The mechanism for our extrication became as much a part of the summit process as did developments in the strategic arms limitation talks that convened in Helsinki in November 1969. In the broadest sense, President Nixon and National Security Adviser Henry Kissinger sought to enlist Soviet interest in assisting the United States in finding an acceptable way to terminate the war in exchange for improved relations between Moscow and Washington. Because of increasingly visible strains in Soviet relations with the People's Republic of China, better relations with Washington were judged to be every bit as important to Soviet interests as finding an end to U.S. intervention in Vietnam was to our own. Both countries would come to find strong motivations for improving their relations, but for fundamentally different reasons.

According to his national security adviser, President Nixon entered the White House convinced like his predecessors, particularly Eisenhower, that a summit meeting with the Soviets could only succeed if it was well-prepared. "His original intention was to use the prospect of a summit only when it could be a means to extract important Soviet concessions."[1]

The first Soviet "feeler" about the prospects for a summit meeting was raised by Ambassador Dobrynin in talks with Kissinger on January 20, 1970, but Kissinger demurred, stating that the timing was not yet right. The two met again in April, and Dobrynin floated the possibility of a meeting when Premier Kosygin attended the opening session of the United Nations in New York; but this was again rejected. Other exchanges continued and on June 23 Dobrynin suggested that the two leaders might want to discuss developments in the Middle East, China and Southeast Asia, as well as European security. It appeared to Kissinger that the Soviets were toying with Nixon's known desires for

---

[1] Henry A. Kissinger, *White House Years* (Boston: Little, Brown & Co., 1979), p. 552.

a summit by proposing a long shopping list of subjects to test the president's eagerness:

> They wanted to be paid in advance for agreeing to the summit and then be paid again at the summit. They tried to obtain a de facto alliance against China, a European Security Conference, and a SALT agreement on their own terms—all as an entrance price into the summit.
>
> Nixon was not that eager. Nor was he incompetent. He agreed to none of these demands, and the Soviets achieved nothing.[2]

Further exchanges about the possibilities of a meeting later in the year continued until September 25, when the Soviets suggested postponing further talk on summit prospects until the following year. The delay upset Nixon, for it meant that our involvement in Vietnam would continue without the prospect of gaining Soviet assistance at a summit for its termination. A month later, on October 22, Dobrynin and Foreign Minister Gromyko met with Nixon, Kissinger, and Secretary of State Rogers, who had not previously been involved in the summit discussions.

Gromyko appeared amenable to the idea of a summit but wanted to see a settlement on the Berlin problem first. A Soviet-FRG agreement had been signed on August 12, 1970, recognizing existing borders, but formal agreement among the wartime allies was still required for settlement. Efforts to resolve that lingering problem were undertaken in January 1971 in talks between Kissinger and Dobrynin in Washington and were directly linked to the prospects for a summit that year by the Soviet ambassador.[3] (Those talks eventually led to the Quadripartite Agreement on Germany of September 3, 1971.) Also in January, President Nixon initiated "back channel" communications with Moscow in

---

[2]Ibid., p. 557.
[3]Ibid., p. 833: "Clearly, if I linked Berlin to SALT, the Soviets linked Berlin to a summit."

an effort to resolve differences and break deadlocks in the strategic arms limitation talks.

Throughout the spring of 1971, summit prospects were alternately connected with progress on SALT, the Berlin situation, and Vietnam. It appeared that both sides were now trying the carrot-and-stick routine, with the summit in the balance. Another effort was made on June 8 to come to agreement on a date for the summit as Kissinger and Dobrynin met at Camp David, but again the details of timing were put off. Shortly after, in early July, Kissinger was off on his "secret trip" to China that resulted in President Nixon's subsequent announcement that he would visit China in February 1972. Moscow's interest in a U.S.-Soviet summit suddenly peaked.[4] On August 10 the president received a formal invitation to visit Moscow for talks in May or June of 1972. After the details were arranged, a joint announcement of the trip was made in Moscow and Washington on October 12.

The president's trip to China clearly marked a historic event of immense significance in the relations between the United States and the People's Republic, as well as in the relationship existing between each of those countries and the Soviet Union. The presidential trip was climaxed by the Shanghai communiqué of February 27, with its declaration that neither country recognized "hegemony" in the area, a phrase that quickly caught Moscow's attention.

A month after this spectacular breakthrough, the North Vietnamese spring offensive began on March 30 with

---

[4]Beam, *Multiple Exposure*, pp. 260-63: "The touchstone to the turn-around in our relations with the Soviets was the president's announcement on July 15, 1971, that he would visit China the following year. . . . On July 28, 1971, I was summoned by Gromyko for a long talk on the state of our relations. . . . Gromyko said that Brezhnev felt that there was a lack of clarity about U.S. intentions, especially toward the Soviet Union. . . . I told Gromyko that I knew Brezhnev's personal interest would be much appreciated in Washington. . . . Thus a path of discussion was confirmed which led inexorably, albeit through some murky episodes, to the May 1972 summit in Moscow."

attacks across the demilitarized zone in Quang Tri prov-
ince. President Nixon retaliated with a resumption of the
bombing of North Vietnam, an action that led, in turn, to
North Vietnam's cancellation on April 15 of talks scheduled for April 24 in Paris. Meanwhile, Kissinger was getting
ready for another "secret trip," this time to Moscow on
April 21–24 to prepare for the forthcoming May summit
meeting. The trip had been suggested by Foreign Minister
Gromyko the previous December for the purpose of
coming to agreement on the proposed agenda, but the
offensive in Vietnam increased the president's determination to link the prospects for the summit to Soviet
willingness to help end the war there. As recounted in
Nixon's memoirs:

> In my conversation with Kissinger and in the instruc-
> tions I sent him in Moscow, I stressed that I wanted him
> to make Vietnam the first order of business and to
> refuse to discuss anything that the Soviets wanted—
> particularly the trade agreements for which they were so
> eager—until they specifically committed themselves to
> help end the war.[5]

Kissinger conveyed the president's message to General
Secretary Brezhnev, who was accompanied by Premier
Kosygin and President Podgorny, as well as Foreign
Minister Gromyko and Ambassador Dobrynin (who had
joined Kissinger on the flight to Moscow). But Kissinger
was unable to get specific assurances from the Soviet
leaders on what measures they would take to help stem the
current offensive. Discussion then turned to other subjects
on the summit's proposed agenda, a development evidently
at variance with Nixon's desires. Whereas the president
wanted to use the threat of cancelling the summit in order
to gain Soviet cooperation on Vietnam, Kissinger judged it
wiser to "shift the risks and the onus for cancellation to the

[5]Richard M. Nixon, *RN, The Memoirs of Richard Nixon* (New York: Grosset &
Dunlap, 1978), p. 587.

Soviets and to use Moscow's eagerness for the summit as a device for separating Moscow from Hanoi."[6] Communication delays and the difference in time zones between Washington and Moscow further aggravated this divergence, as later recounted by Kissinger, but the talks did result in an agenda that was acceptable to both sides.

To minimize the potential for "leaks" from these discussions, Kissinger used a Soviet interpreter. It was only after their completion that he made known his presence in Moscow to U.S. Ambassador Jacob Beam and provided him with a "back-briefing" of the results. Earlier, on March 14, Secretary of State Rogers had sent a memorandum to the president stating that he intended to "take personal charge" of the summit preparations; but Nixon responded to the effect that all major preparations would be supervised by the national security adviser.[7]

With the subsequent failure of Kissinger's secret meeting with Le Duc Tho in Paris on May 2 to make any progress on the mounting hostilities in Vietnam, the president was facing the predicament of negotiating with the Soviets in Moscow at the same time they were supporting the Vietnamese offensive. The prospects for a summit failure of the type Eisenhower experienced in Paris in 1960 obviously came to mind. If there was to be any cancellation of the Moscow summit, he wanted to initiate it.[8] Caught in the

---

[6]Kissinger, *White House Years*, p. 1154. President Nixon's account is as follows: "We were ... completely agreed on our overall strategy and goals as he prepared for his trip to Moscow. However, his opinion on the tactics he should follow in his talks was somewhat different from mine.... [He] continued to feel that flexibility must be the cornerstone of any successful negotiation, and he urged me to let him feel out the situation rather than risk everything by imposing any rigid preconditions." Nixon, *Memoirs*, pp. 587-88.

[7]Kissinger, *White House Years*, p. 1128.

[8]In a memorandum to Kissinger, the president wrote: "... I intend to cancel the Summit unless the situation militarily and diplomatically substantially improves by May 15 at the latest or unless we get a firm commitment from the Russians to announce a joint agreement at the summit to use our influence to end the war." Nixon, *Memoirs*, pp. 593-94.

bind, Nixon decided on May 8 on a resumption of the bombing of Hanoi and mining of Haiphong Harbor. As recalled in his memoirs, the president had observed at the time: "'... The summit isn't worth a damn if the price for it is losing in Vietnam. My instinct tells me that the country can take losing the summit, but it can't take losing the war.'"[9] Such was the context in which the first Nixon-Brezhnev summit convened two weeks later.

After a chilly reception in Moscow and various tirades against the bombing and mining of North Vietnam's harbors, the summit was a success, as exemplified most notably in two agreements: the Treaty on Anti-Ballistic Missile Systems, which limited each country to the construction of two systems; and the Interim Agreement on Limitation of Strategic Offensive Arms, which stated that neither country would start construction of additional land-based ICBM launchers after July 1, 1972, thus freezing their levels to the numbers deployed and under construction at the time. The Protocol to that Interim Agreement further specified, inter alia, that the U.S. was limited to 710 submarine ballistic missile launchers on 44 modern submarines, and the Soviet Union to 950 launchers on 62 modern submarines, along with a provision for trade-offs on replacements for SLBMs (submarine-launched ballistic missiles) on older-type submarines.

This agreement, later dubbed SALT I, was the culmination of a long process. Three years earlier, President Nixon had decided to resume the efforts initiated by President Johnson at the Glassboro summit for formal strategic arms limitation talks with the Soviets, and these commenced in November of 1969 at Helsinki. They continued for the next two and a half years in Vienna and Geneva under the direction of Ambassador Gerard C. Smith, director of the Arms Control and Disarmament

---

[9]Ibid., p. 602.

Agency, and his Soviet counterpart, Deputy Foreign Minister Vladimir Semenov, who was assisted by Colonel-General Ogarkov, first deputy chief of the General Staff of the Armed Forces.

Throughout the early stages of the negotiations, delegations consisting of about ten people on each side conducted meetings twice weekly, followed by informal sessions. Subsequently, the U.S. side took to preparing MEMCONs ("memoranda of conversations") numbering over five hundred in the 2½-year period. These were dispatched to the SALT community in Washington, consisting of about fifty government experts, mostly in the Departments of State and Defense, as well as in the Arms Control and Disarmament Agency.[10] National Security Adviser Kissinger kept track of their progress through meetings of the Verification Panel, the group he chaired to review the inspection or "policing" arrangements, and significant problems were occasionally brought to the attention of the National Security Council. Then, in addition (and as previously noted), President Nixon began the "back-channel" correspondence with Kosygin in January 1971, which was supplemented by the Kissinger-Dobrynin talks. (After the Twenty-fourth Party Congress in April 1971, Brezhnev began to replace Kosygin as the Kremlin's chief spokesman and by 1972 became the recipient of the back-channel communications.)[11]

In sum, then, there were four different levels of arms control discussions going on at the same time: formal plenary and informal sessions between the SALT teams; the Kissinger-Dobrynin talks; and the "back channel" between Washington and Moscow. Neither Ambassador Smith nor Secretary Rogers was informed of the back

---

[10]Raymond L. Garthoff, "Negotiating SALT," *The Wilson Quarterly* (Autumn 1977), p. 78.

[11]Ibid., p. 80, and Garthoff, "Negotiating with the Russians: Some Lessons from SALT," *International Security*, Vol. 1, No. 4 (Spring 1977), p. 6.

channel, however, until the day before President Nixon's announcement of May 20 that an agreement had been reached with the Soviets to separate the ABM treaty from related progress on offensive weapons limitations, in effect a major breakthrough in the deadlocked negotiations.[12]

The fact that the SALT negotiations were proceeding at all, let alone making significant progress, dates back to fundamental agreement between the two sides in 1968 on the common objectives and conceptual framework to be employed during the process.[13] The emphasis of the main objective was on the need for strategic stability, and that required limitation of offensive weapons if deterrence was to be effective for either side. It was agreed that neither side should be allowed a military advantage, and agreements would be based on parity in nuclear weaponry. And it was agreed that further measures were required to reduce the risk of nuclear war from miscalculation or accident.

These principles, however, led to contrasting approaches once the negotiations commenced, as observed in the following passage from a congressional study:

> The Soviets and the Americans approached SALT from two markedly different negotiating concepts: the Soviets from the general; the Americans from the specific. The conflict in approaches made negotiations even more difficult than ordinarily would have been the case. The Soviets wanted a general politically meaningful accord. They sought "agreement in principle" prior to agreement on specifics. Their approach was directed at a general American acceptance of a rough parity already achieved and a more general restraint in the military buildup while emphasizing political détente.

---

[12]Ibid., p. 80.

[13]When President Johnson signed the Nuclear Non-Proliferation Treaty in Washington, D.C. on July 1, 1968, he announced that agreement had been reached with the Soviets to hold strategic arms talks. This was the "first step" in the process. The next step was to find an agreed time and place for the negotiations. The Soviet invasion of Czechoslovakia in mid-August of that year, however, prevented further progress at the time. Johnson, *Vantage Point*, pp. 485-90.

In contrast, the American approach was pragmatic. It began with the specifics. It offered a fairly complete, complex, and detailed package proposal. It focused on concrete, militarily meaningful measures for arms control. It stressed specific measures reflecting "fine tuning" adjustments in the military balance in order to enhance strategic stability and mutual deterrence.[14]

The joint announcement in Moscow and Washington on October 12, 1971 of agreement to hold the summit meeting in May 1972 put additional pressures on the SALT negotiators to come to terms with remaining issues. By the time the summit convened, there were three such outstanding problems: 1) the distance permitted between the two ABM systems that would be allowed; 2) what increases in size or volume, if any, would be permitted for ICBMs and their silos; and 3) what submarine-launched ballistic missiles (SLBMs) to count (i.e., the SLBMs on new versus older submarines).[15] Resolution of these matters became the principal task of President Nixon and Kissinger at the summit meeting. The president would negotiate directly with General Secretary Brezhnev on these details, a task that he felt was befitting the leaders of the two countries.[16]

Kissinger, with assistance by NSC staff members Helmut Sonnenfeldt and William Hyland (both Soviet experts), coordinated developments with Gromyko and his aides and with the U.S. SALT delegation that remained stationed in Helsinki. Efforts at the latter were "astonishingly cumbersome," as recalled by Kissinger later, and he judged that it would have been better to have the SALT teams in

---

[14]U.S. Congress, *Soviet Diplomacy and Negotiating Behavior: Emerging New Context for U.S. Diplomacy*, op. cit., p. 459. See also Garthoff, "Negotiating SALT," pp. 81-82, and his "Negotiating with the Russians," p. 5.

[15]Kissinger, *White House Years*, pp. 1217-19.

[16]Nixon, *Memoirs*, p. 592, states the following: "Having reached this impasse, Kissinger proceeded to move on to further discussions of summit agenda items. He was able to arrange the entire agenda except for the most sensitive elements of SALT, which would require direct negotiation between Brezhnev and me."

Moscow to work in synchronization with the summit proceedings.[17] In addition to coordinating problems on issues of substance, particularly on SLBM matters, communications with Helsinki were awkward at best. Messages from Helsinki went through State Department channels with a copy to the U.S. Embassy in Moscow, which was then delivered to the administrative headquarters set up in the Hotel Rossiya, and finally taken to the Kremlin where Nixon and Kissinger stayed during the summit. Evidently some "bugging" problems there necessitated the use of a "scrambler," further compounding the difficulties.[18]

Among the various meetings between Nixon and Brezhnev, which often shifted in composition depending on subject matter, there were a number of private sessions in which the only other person present was a Soviet interpreter, Viktor Sukhodrev. That procedure was subsequently questioned, since it deprived the U.S. of transcripts of the discussions and later gave rise to suspicions of "secret agreements" being reached between the two leaders. Based on other meetings in which he participated, Kissinger later concluded:

> The meetings demonstrated that heads of government should not negotiate complex subjects. Neither Brezhnev nor Nixon had mastered the technical issues; both were lagging hours behind the delegations in Helsinki, who were going merrily ahead on the very same points.[19]

The summit put pressures on the negotiations to finalize agreements in time for signature by the principals, which resulted in some hastily concluded SALT documents. The SLBM portion of the Interim Agreement, contained in the

---

[17]Kissinger, *White House Years*, pp. 1129-30.

[18]The "scrambler" was used in an attempt to thwart Soviet "bugging" of their rooms in the Kremlin. On sensitive matters, Nixon and Kissinger would take refuge in their official car or go for a walk.

[19]Kissinger, *White House Years*, p. 1220.

Protocol to that agreement, has been cited most often as an example; it apparently had to be done over after signature and signed again by the leaders a day or two later.

Among the other agreements signed, which covered such matters as environmental protection, medical science and public health, cooperation in space, science and technology, and prevention of incidents at sea, the one entitled Basic Principles of Relations Between the United States of America and the Union of Soviet Socialist Republics was of special significance to Moscow. Soviet interest in such an agreement was initially raised by Ambassador Dobrynin in his talks with Kissinger in Washington, and its consummation at the summit was construed in Moscow as symbolizing U.S. recognition of the Soviet Union as a co-equal superpower. Although this agreement was generally devoid of operative content, Kissinger observed that

> ... the fundamental achievement was to sketch the outline on which coexistence between the democracies and the Soviet system must be based. SALT embodied our conviction that a wildly spiraling nuclear arms race was in no country's interest and enhanced no one's security; the "Basic Principles" gave at least verbal expression to the necessity of responsible political conduct. The two elements reinforced each other; they symbolized our conviction that a relaxation of tensions could not be based exclusively on arms control; the ultimate test would be restrained international behavior.[20]

One final aspect of the Moscow summit proceedings concerns what has since been called the "shock tactics" employed by Soviet leaders in their informal talks with Nixon and Kissinger.[21] After Brezhnev somewhat impulsively spirited the president away from the Kremlin for a hydrofoil ride on the Moscow River, the principals re-

---

[20]Ibid., pp. 1253-54.
[21]See, for example, Nixon, *Memoirs*, pp. 611-14.

grouped at his dacha for discussions and dinner. But the festive mood suddenly changed into a confrontation over Vietnam and the recent round of B-52 bombings of Hanoi and Haiphong the president had ordered just before the summit. Brezhnev lambasted Nixon for the "barbaric act" of mining the North Vietnamese harbors and this was followed with similar attacks by President Podgorny and Premier Kosygin. And, just as suddenly as the mood had turned sour, the tirade abruptly ended when the leaders went to a later-than-expected dinner, where Soviet hospitality and conviviality returned. The Vietnam session was, apparently, a pro forma performance for the Soviets. Nixon later remarked that it reminded him of Dr. Jekyll and Mr. Hyde.[22]

A joint communiqué was released on May 29. It was all but complete before the summit took place, as Kissinger and Dobrynin had started work on it in Washington. There was only one major area of disagreement to be settled and that concerned the Middle East. The Soviets wanted a strong statement on joint efforts to achieve peace in the region; but, unwilling to open the door to further Soviet involvement and influence in the Middle East, Kissinger would agree only to a bland statement on the matter. He later attributed President Sadat's expulsion of Soviet advisers in July of that year to Moscow's inability to achieve more for its Arab client state at the summit.[23]

Upon the president's return to Washington on June 1, he immediately reported to Congress that "the foundation has been laid for a new relationship between the two most powerful nations in the world."[24] Kissinger's assessment was as follows:

---

[22]Ibid., p. 613.

[23]Kissinger, *White House Years*, p. 1248.

[24]President Nixon's Address to Congress on June 1, 1972, "The Moscow Summit: New Opportunities in U.S.-Soviet Relations," reprinted in U.S. Department of State, *Bulletin*, Vol. 66, No. 1722 (June 26, 1972), p. 855.

The context as well as the content of the summit made it a major success for American foreign policy. The fact that we had faced down Hanoi and yet completed major negotiations with Moscow . . . evoked the prospect of a more hopeful future and thus put Vietnam into perspective. The summits helped us complete the isolation of Hanoi by giving Moscow and Peking a stake in their ties with us. What was even more novel, we were freed for the better part of the year from the domestic turmoil on which thus far Hanoi had always been able to count. This, together with the military defeat of the North Vietnamese offensive, led to a breakthrough in the peace negotiations within months. The summit was equally significant for the evolution of the Middle East. . . . [I]t marked a turning point at which moderate Arab leaders began to move toward Washington. . . . [25]

The Anti-Ballistic Missile Systems Treaty was approved by the Senate Foreign Relations Committee and endorsed 88-2 by the full Senate on August 3. The Interim Agreement passed both houses of Congress in September, and on the 30th of that month the president signed the joint resolution authorizing approval of the Interim Agreement and Protocol thereto. Both accords then became effective on October 3rd with the exchange of ratifications.[26]

Brezhnev's Visit to the U.S., June 18–25, 1973

NEGOTIATIONS FOR A SALT II agreement commenced six months after the Moscow summit. In October 1972 a trade agreement was signed in Washington at the same time that the old Lend-Lease debt problem was finally resolved by compromise on both the U.S. and Soviet sides.[27] But some misgivings began to surface on the SALT

---

[25]Kissinger, *White House Years*, p. 1253.

[26]U.S. Congress, *Soviet Diplomacy and Negotiating Behavior: Emerging New Context for U.S. Diplomacy*, p. 484.

[27]Beam, *Multiple Exposure*, pp. 287-88, states that the Most-Favored-Nation

agreements, particularly about whether the U.S. had accepted a "second-best" position with regard to the SLBM figures. Instructions to the U.S. SALT negotiating team in Geneva became confused because of the controversy and represented "a melange" of differing positions from the departments and agencies.[28] As the talks resumed in early 1973, Kissinger prepared to undertake another trip to Moscow to arrange the details for Brezhnev's return visit to the United States in June, as had been approved at the Moscow summit. Prior to doing so, however, he made further progress with the Chinese on a visit to Peking in February 1973, which resulted in agreement to set up liaison offices in the two capitals to further efforts at a normalization in Sino-American relations. Earlier, in late January 1973, the Agreement on Ending the War and Restoring Peace in Vietnam had been signed. The combination of improved relations with China and an end in sight for the Vietnam agonies placed the next summit with Brezhnev in a new light from the American perspective. As related by Kissinger: "We were becoming confident that we would be free of the Vietnam war by 1973; a summit was no longer important to separate Moscow from Hanoi."[29]

On his trip to Moscow on May 4-9, Kissinger met with Brezhnev and Gromyko at the Politburo hunting retreat in Zavidovo. Brezhnev stressed the need for agreement on a treaty for the prevention of nuclear war and warned that U.S. military assistance to China was a matter of grave concern that could lead to war. His concern with a nuclear treaty had been conveyed on February 21, 1973 in a letter to

---

(MFN) status was conditioned on settlement of the Lend-Lease account and that in the 1950s the U.S. demanded $10 billion to settle that but compromised at $722 million when both agreements were signed in Washington, D.C. on October 18, 1972.

[28]Henry Kissinger, *Years of Upheaval* (Boston: Little, Brown and Co., 1982), p. 271.

[29]Ibid., p. 279.

Nixon,[30] and Gromyko had indicated that Brezhnev's trip would be conditional on progress toward such a treaty. But what was emerging at Zavidovo reflected Soviet purposes more clearly, as revealed in Kissinger's account:

> It would have been difficult to draw up a more bald or cynical definition of condominium. The proposed treaty would protect the superpowers against nuclear destruction even in a European war while guaranteeing the devastation of each country's allies. Nothing would have been better designed to promote European neutralism or to depreciate the value of alliances.[31]

In any event, the Agreement on the Prevention of Nuclear War that was signed by Nixon and Brezhnev in Washington on June 22, 1973 was quite different than that originally intended by the Kremlin. Despite Soviet efforts for a nuclear condominium, the United States was less pressed by Vietnam now and could afford to stall on the agreement until Moscow was willing to accept a watered-down version of their original objectives. Article IV of the treaty simply stated that the two powers would undertake urgent consultations whenever the risks of nuclear conflict appeared in their relations, or in their relations with other countries.[32] The wording of the agreement had been worked out during Kissinger's Zavidovo visit and required no further negotiations before signature at the summit meeting.

General Secretary Brezhnev had arrived in Washington on June 16 and rested at Camp David before meeting with the president, on June 18, for the start of talks and his official visit. After a welcoming ceremony on the White

---

[30]Ibid., p. 280.

[31]Ibid., p. 277.

[32]As observed by Kissinger, the Agreement on the Prevention of Nuclear War was invoked once in the decade after its signature: during the Middle East alert of 1973, when the U.S. warned the Soviets that their unilateral intervention would violate its provisions. Ibid., p. 286.

House lawn, he and Nixon met privately for discussions, using the translation services of the Soviet interpreter Viktor Sukhodrov, just as they had done the previous year in Moscow. The purpose of the meeting was to agree on the agenda, but Secretary Rogers, Kissinger and Sonnenfeldt, who were waiting outside the Oval Office to join in the discussion, were not invited in nor informed of the substance of the talks. Later, in his memoirs, President Nixon stated that Brezhnev's purpose at that initial meeting was to impress upon the president that the U.S.-Soviet relationship was far more important than the emerging relations between the United States and China.[33] He also repeated his warnings about the consequences of U.S. military assistance to China.

After an exchange of official dinners in Washington and further discussions at Camp David on June 20, Brezhnev joined the president at the "Western White House" in San Clemente. Official meetings in all three locations followed a haphazard pattern that necessitated last-minute changes in the personnel lineup, and meetings were sometimes cancelled for no apparent reason when Soviet participants simply did not show up.

As the president's house guest in San Clemente, Brezhnev became more informal and more amenable to meaningful and candid talks. After a convivial dinner on the last evening of the visit, however, Brezhnev returned to the "shock tactics" employed at the Moscow summit and informed Nixon at 10:30 p.m. that he wanted to talk some more. For the next three hours, the Soviet leader harangued the president on the necessity for a Middle East settlement based on Arab demands and Israeli withdrawal from occupied territories under pressure from the United States. As related by Nixon:

---

[33]Nixon, *Memoirs*, p. 878.

This testy midnight session was a reminder of the unchanging and unrelenting Communist motivations beneath the diplomatic veneer of détente.... From his point of view, therefore, his use of shock tactics at the ostensibly impromptu meeting in my study in San Clemente was a calculated risk. Brezhnev could not seriously have expected me to rise to the meager bait he held out in return for what would amount to our abandoning Israel. Whether he already had a commitment to the Arabs to support an attack against Israel is not clear, but I am confident that the firmness I showed that night reinforced the seriousness of the message I conveyed to the Soviets when I ordered a military alert four months later during the Yom Kippur War.[34]

The joint communiqué signed the following morning simply reflected differing views on the Middle East and was not otherwise noteworthy for its substance. But the leaders did establish the end of 1974 as the target date for signature of a treaty on the limitation of strategic offensive missiles. And they had consummated on June 21 in Washington an Agreement on the Basic Principles of Negotiation on Strategic Arms Limitation, which included a pledge to continue active negotiations toward that end based on explicit recognition of each other's "equal security interests."[35] A host of other agreements were signed during this 1973 summit on such matters as cooperation in transportation, agriculture, oceanic studies, taxation, commercial aviation, trade, and the peaceful uses of atomic energy.

While these agreements were not as noteworthy as the SALT I agreements at the 1972 Moscow summit, the

---

[34]Ibid., p. 885.

[35]As stated in the Agreement on Basic Principles: " ... both Sides will be guided by the recognition of each other's equal security interests and by the recognition that efforts to obtain unilateral advantage, directly or indirectly, would be inconsistent with the strengthening of peaceful relations.... " The text of the Agreement is reprinted in U.S. Department of State, *Bulletin*, Vol. 69, No. 1778 (July 23, 1973), p. 158.

president noted their importance in the larger context of bilateral relations: "These continued the process that we had begun in 1972 of building an interlocking web of relationships to increase the Soviets' stake in stability and cooperation."[36] Moreover, since virtually all of these had been negotiated ahead of time, the thirty-five hours the two leaders did have together during the visit could be devoted to frank talks to explore each other's minds—"the best use of summit diplomacy," according to Kissinger.[37]

The Moscow Summit and State Visit, June 27–July 3, 1974

THE WATERGATE INVESTIGATION had been only an annoying distraction during Brezhnev's visit (John Dean had been scheduled to testify before Senator Sam Ervin's Senate Select Committee the very week of the visit, but that was postponed). At the time of his final summit meeting with Brezhnev in 1974, however, President Nixon was so fully enmeshed in Watergate that the summit meeting could have been called a success for its very occurrence, let alone its substantive results.

As before, the invitation for the return visit had been extended and accepted during the preceding visit, in this case Brezhnev's, and the prospect of an annual U.S.-Soviet summit meeting was now becoming part of the routine in bilateral relations. Also as before, Henry Kissinger was dispatched to Moscow in late March 1974 to arrange the details of the summit. But the timing and circumstances were anything but routine, as Kissinger later recounted:

> It was not a propitious time. Nixon's plight became more apparent with every day. The Soviets were being squeezed to the sidelines in the Syrian disengagement

---

[36]Nixon, *Memoirs*, p. 886.
[37]Kissinger, *Years of Upheaval*, p. 289.

negotiations; obstacles to U.S.-Soviet trade were multi-
plying from unexpected quarters.... With Watergate
raging, MFN deadlocked, détente and SALT becoming
increasingly controversial, it was not a glorious moment
to negotiate with the Soviets.[38]

The president, crippled by Watergate and attacked by
what he called "anti-détente" forces under Senator
Jackson's leadership, was hardly in a position to negotiate
further agreement on strategic arms limitations in preparation for the summit. In fact, Kissinger later stated that
"Jackson and others in the anti-détente lobby were determined that Nixon should have no negotiating chips in
Moscow."[39] At a National Security Council meeting on
June 20, one week after Paul Nitze resigned as the
Department of Defense representative on the SALT delegation, Defense Secretary Schlesinger presented the Penta-
gon's position. Nixon called it "an unyielding hard line
against any SALT agreement that did not ensure an
overwhelming American advantage."[40]

Disagreement on U.S. objectives centered on increasingly arcane concepts of "equal aggregates" versus
"counterbalancing asymmetries," dealing with how to
come to terms with measuring U.S. and Soviet nuclear
missile capabilities. Concluded Strobe Talbott in *Deadly
Gambits*:

> While Kissinger saw Schlesinger as hung up on throw-
> weight, Schlesinger felt that Kissinger was excessively
> concerned with what was negotiable and not enough
> with what was strategically desirable. He suspected that
> Kissinger was pandering to Richard Nixon's despera-
> tion for a SALT II agreement in 1974 as part of his
> campaign to deflect attention from the Watergate
> scandal. As it happened, Watergate swept aside the
> Nixon presidency and, along with it, any chance of a

---

[38]Ibid., p. 994.
[39]Ibid., p. 997.
[40]Nixon, *Memoirs*, p. 1024.

SALT II breakthrough at the Moscow summit in 1974.[41]

The beleaguered president left Washington on June 25 for a stop in Brussels to attend ceremonies celebrating the 25th anniversary of NATO and to sign the Declaration on Atlantic Relations. Upon his departure from Andrews Air Force Base, he had stated that his purposes at the summit were threefold: 1) to strengthen bilateral relations with the Soviets; 2) to develop further areas of cooperation to displace confrontation; and 3) to limit the threat of nuclear arms.[42] His official visit to the Soviet Union would include a trip to Minsk, capital of Byelorussia, and the southern coast of the Crimea, in addition to his talks in Moscow and his address to the Soviet people on July 2.

In terms of substance, the summit produced the Protocol to the Treaty on the Limitation of Anti-Ballistic Missile Systems, which reduced the number of ABM systems from two to one for each country, and the Treaty and Protocol on the Limitation of Underground Nuclear Weapon Tests, essentially restricting such testing to yields of less than 150 kilotons. Other agreements signed included further co-operative efforts on economic, industrial, and technical matters and energy, housing, and artificial heart research. But there was no progress on the subject of limitations on strategic offensive missiles; the most that can be said in that regard is that the two leaders agreed to resume negotiations on the subject at a "mini-summit" before the end of 1974. Upon his return to the United States on July 3, the president stated that although the two sides had not reached a final accord, they were now firmly committed to the resolution of remaining differences.

---

[41]Strobe Talbott, *Deadly Gambits*, p. 218.

[42]President Nixon's departure remarks at Andrews Air Force Base, June 25, 1974, reprinted in U.S. Department of State, *Bulletin*, Vol. 71, No. 1831, (July 29, 1974), p. 165.

In retrospect, President Nixon considered the summit a "mixed bag" and made the following entry in his diary afterward:

> I am inclined to think that in arranging the next summit, it's the informal meetings that provide the greatest opportunity for progress. I think the formal ones—the plenary sessions—produce the least, because everybody's talking for the record and making a record. ... The larger the group, the less free the conversation is. That is something that is true in all forms of society, but it is particularly true in the Soviet Union and in the Communist states.[43]

Kissinger, who at the time was acting in the capacity of both secretary of state and assistant to the president for national security affairs, considered the summit more successful than anticipated. The leaders had ample opportunity for serious discussions about the international situation and were not under pressures or expectations to produce another spectacular signing ceremony, as at the previous Moscow summit. As he saw it:

> The strange thing was that by all normal criteria, the summit had been a success. Significant agreements had been signed—not so earthshaking as on previous occasions but the sort of accords that showed that the superpowers took progress in their relationship seriously.[44]

But the time for further progress ran out with President Nixon's resignation in August. The three summits that had given rise to a period of temporary détente began to recede into the past, as U.S.-Soviet relations again began to decline.

---

[43]Nixon, *Memoirs*, p. 1037.
[44]Kissinger, *Years of Upheaval*, p. 1177.

5

The Vladivostok and Vienna Summits

Ford and Brezhnev at Vladivostok, November 23–24, 1974

A T THE 1974 Moscow summit, President Nixon and General Secretary Brezhnev had agreed to hold a "mini-summit" before the end of the year for the sole purpose of making progress on limitation of offensive strategic missiles. In the wake of Nixon's resignation in August, it became desirable to reaffirm the continuity of U.S. cooperative ties with the Soviet Union and to continue the SALT process. President Ford dispatched Secretary Kissinger to Moscow in October to make preparations for the forthcoming summit meeting that the new president had discussed with Foreign Minister Gromyko at a September meeting of the two in Washington. A week before the Kissinger trip Ford had sent Brezhnev a proposal calling for equal overall levels of offensive missiles, to be set at 2,200 launchers, of which only 1,320 could be equipped with multiple independently-targeted reentry vehicles (MIRVs).[1]

---

[1]Raymond L. Garthoff, *Détente and Confrontation: American-Soviet Relations from Nixon to Reagan* (Washington, D.C.: The Brookings Institution, 1985), p. 443.

Kissinger visited Moscow from October 23 to 27 and was accompanied by State Department officials Helmut Sonnenfeldt, Arthur Hartman, Alfred Atherton, William Hyland, and Winston Lord and National Security Council staff members Jan Lodal and Dennis Clift. The U.S. Ambassador to the Soviet Union, Walter J. Stoessel, Jr., joined in the talks in Moscow with Brezhnev, Gromyko, Dobrynin, and other Soviet officials. As stated in their communiqué of October 27, "particular attention was given to the problem of further limitation of strategic arms" with the fundamental understanding that a new long-term agreement was to be developed to follow up on the 1972 Interim Agreement.[2] There was no announcement that any agreement on the specifics had been reached, only that the discussions would continue and that a working meeting between the president and the general secretary would be held in the vicinity of Vladivostok in November, as both leaders had announced the day before. This summit meeting was timed to coincide with President Ford's previously announced intentions to visit Japan from November 18 to 22 and Korea on the 22nd and 23rd.

President Ford described in his memoirs how he prepared for the meeting:

> Before my meeting with Brezhnev, Kissinger and I talked at length about the Soviet leader's personality and negotiating techniques. Brezhnev, Henry said, would dominate the Soviet side of the discussions, but on technical points he would confer with his advisers. Invariably, Henry continued, he would lead off with an angry, blustery diatribe accusing the U.S. of sabotaging the chances for lasting peace. He would, for example, blame us for not working with the Soviets in the Middle East. But this would be primarily for home consumption. It would give him a chance to score points with the

---

[2]"Communiqué," issued at Moscow, October 27, 1974. Reprinted in U.S. Department of State, *Bulletin*, Vol. 71, No. 1848 (November 25, 1974), p. 703.

Soviet hierarchy. It would also be his way of testing my resolve. He would be curious to see if I would bend or fight back. And so, Henry maintained, we should not retreat from our position. We should be polite but firm. If they really wanted an agreement, they would be the ones to bend. Which is precisely what transpired.[3]

The Vladivostok talks took place at a small resort town, Okeanskaya, in the rather spartan environment of a hastily improvised health spa, located about 65 miles away from where Air Force One had landed. The official parties were essentially the same as noted above during Kissinger's Moscow trip, although Lieutenant General Brent Scowcroft, deputy assistant to the president for national security affairs, joined the U.S. side, and two Soviet generals and two interpreters joined Brezhnev's group.

The first day's discussions focused on the status of the SALT negotiations and efforts to establish the upper limit to the number of offensive missiles that would be permitted to each side under any new agreement. The Soviets insisted on a level higher than the 2,200 limit that Ford had proposed,[4] while the emphasis of the U.S. side was on getting Soviet agreement to an "equal aggregate" number of strategic offensive launchers (ICBMs, SLBMs and heavy bombers).[5] A compromise was then negotiated that set an upper limit of 2,400 strategic launchers for both sides, with a sublimit of 1,320 missiles that could be equipped with MIRVs.

Brezhnev attempted to get Ford to agree that U.S. forward-based systems (FBS) in Europe (consisting of nuclear weapons and F-4s, F-111s and FB-111s) should be included be in the U.S. count of the aggregate number, but this was rejected by Ford. Brezhnev also tried without

---

[3]Gerald R. Ford, *A Time to Heal* (New York: Harper & Row, 1979), pp. 215-16.

[4]Ibid., p. 216.

[5]Garthoff, *Détente and Confrontation*, p. 446.

success to get U.S. programs for the Trident submarine and B-1 bomber stopped. U.S. efforts to get the Soviet "Back-fire" bomber to count against their aggregate became a "definitional ambiguity," as put by one observer,[6] and were shrouded in the more general phraseology of "heavy bomber" that was used at Vladivostok. These results of the Vladivostok meeting became the framework within which SALT negotiations would resume in January 1975 in Geneva, with the intent of producing a new agreement that would incorporate the provisions of the 1972 Interim Agreement and be effective from October 1977 to December 31, 1985.

These points, including the 1975 Geneva meeting date, were specified in the Joint Statement on Strategic Offensive Arms, issued on November 24 from Vladivostok.[7] That statement further reaffirmed agreement that the basis of the negotiations and treaties would rest on the "principle of equality and equal security" for both countries. The more perplexing problem of whether U.S.-developed cruise missiles should be included in the SALT calculations was not addressed in either the Joint Statement or the Joint Communiqué.

The second day's discussions focused on international issues but achieved no significant breakthroughs. It was agreed that settlement of the Cyprus crisis would be based upon implementation of measures adopted by the U.N. Security Council and General Assembly; that the Middle East was still regarded as a "dangerous situation" and that a just and lasting peace there would be promoted on the basis of U.N. Resolution 338; and that both sides placed high importance on negotiations on mutual and balanced

---

[6]Strobe Talbott, *Endgame—The Inside Story of SALT II* (New York: Harper & Row, 1979), p. 33.

[7]"Joint Statement on Strategic Offensive Arms," Vladivostok, November 24, 1974, reprinted in U.S. Department of State, *Bulletin*, Vol. 71, No. 1852 (December 23, 1974), p. 879.

force reduction in Europe and progress at the Conference on Security and Cooperation in Europe.[8] The two leaders endorsed further cooperative ties in commercial and economic matters, as well as in scientific, technological and cultural exchanges. The Joint Communiqué reaffirmed "the practical value of Soviet-American summit meetings and their exceptional importance in the shaping of a new relationship" between the U.S. and the Soviet Union.[9]

Upon his return to Washington, President Ford's arrival remarks at Andrews Air Force Base on November 24 were optimistic. He stated that his meeting with General Secretary Brezhnev went "very, very well."[10] (Later, in his memoirs, he stated that the meetings had exceeded his expectations.)[11] He announced the details of the SALT framework at a news conference on December 2 and emphasized that a cap had finally been put on the arms race.

Helsinki 1975. President Ford had another occasion to meet with General Secretary Brezhnev the following year on July 30 and August 2 in Helsinki, where the leaders from thirty-five nations had assembled for the signing of the Final Act of the Conference on Security and Cooperation in Europe. Ford and Brezhnev held two meetings, which were centered on problems with further progress on the SALT negotiations in Geneva, specifically those relating to verification measures, cruise missiles, and the Backfire bomber.[12] The subject of a return visit by Brezhnev to the

---

[8]"Joint Communiqué" signed at Vladivostok on November 24, 1974, in ibid., p. 881.

[9]Ibid.

[10]President Ford's arrival remarks at Andrews Air Force Base, November 24, 1974, in ibid., p. 882.

[11]Ford, *A Time to Heal*, p. 218.

[12]Ibid., pp. 303-6. See also excerpts from President Ford's question-and-answer session with reporters aboard Air Force One on August 2, 1975, in U.S. Department of State, *Bulletin*, Vol. 73, No. 1888 (September 1, 1975), pp. 308-11. In addition to attending the CSCE ceremonies and meeting with Brezhnev in

United States, possibly in the fall, was raised by reporters, but Secretary Kissinger linked that to progress on the SALT discussions in Geneva.[13]

Both Ford and Brezhnev said their brief meetings were productive and businesslike, and they agreed that Secretary Kissinger and Foreign Minister Gromyko should pursue areas of disagreement more fully to refine the remaining obstacles to completion of the SALT accord agreed upon at Vladivostok. But even if these technical problems had been resolved, it is questionable whether or not further progress on final agreement could have been made at that time. The context within which they were proceeding—both internationally and domestically, in the United States—was also undergoing fundamental changes that were at odds with the SALT process, and with détente in general.

The year 1975 was marked by the collapse of Saigon in April and the realities of America's lost cause and war in Vietnam. Governmental indecision in Washington was seized upon by the Soviets with their airlift of Cuban troops into Angola and, subsequently, into the Horn of Africa. And relations between Moscow and Washington soured in that year with Soviet rejection of the trade agreements wrought by the Nixon-Brezhnev summits, because of what the Soviets considered unwarranted interference in their internal affairs by the U.S. Congress.[14] The cases in point were the Jackson-Vanik amendment to the Trade Act, which specifically linked granting the Soviet Union most-favored-nation (MFN) status to increased levels of Jewish emigration, and the Stevenson amendment, which limited loans from the Export-Import Bank to the Soviet Union to $300 million. On January 15, 1975 Secretary Kissinger

---

Helsinki, he visited the Federal Republic of Germany on July 26-28, Poland on July 28-29, Romania on August 2-3, and Yugoslavia on August 3-4.

[13]Secretary Kissinger's news conferences in Helsinki on July 30 and 31, 1975, ibid., pp. 313-14.

[14]As expressed in a letter of October 26, 1974 from Gromyko to Kissinger. See Beam, *Multiple Exposure*, p. 289.

announced that the Soviets would not put the 1972 trade agreements into force.[15]

In the election year of 1976, President Ford faced a groundswell of conservative reactions in his primary nomination battle with Ronald Reagan, forcing him to shelve efforts to reach agreement on a framework for SALT II for fear of being labelled "soft on communism" by the challenger. Seeing the whole concept of détente and SALT under attack, Ford even banished official use of the term 'détente' in administration statements. Jimmy Carter's election on November 2, 1976, however, brought a new unknown factor into the SALT process that Moscow would have to assess.

Carter and Brezhnev at Vienna,
June 15–18, 1979

IN HIS INAUGURAL address, President Carter pledged to work toward the elimination of nuclear weapons as his ultimate goal. As a first step, he directed the National Security Council staff and the State and Defense Departments to evolve proposals that would change the emphasis in future SALT negotiations from "limitation" to "reduction". He wrote Brezhnev on January 26, 1977 to inform him of the seriousness with which he viewed arms control and met with Ambassador Dobrynin six days later in the Oval Office to discuss, among other things, his proposals for "deep cuts" in the total number of nuclear weapons. These were conveyed to Brezhnev in a second letter on February 14, 1977. In his reply of February 25, the Soviet leader characterized the proposals as "deliberately unacceptable" because of their variance with the framework established at Vladivostok.[16]

---

[15]Ibid.
[16]Jimmy Carter, *Keeping Faith* (New York: Bantam Books, 1982), p. 218.

After another exchange of letters, President Carter decided to send Secretary of State Vance to Moscow with three proposals that had been approved at a National Security Council meeting on March 22. The first option, and the one most strongly favored by the president, again called for "deep cuts," reducing the levels of strategic launchers agreed to at Vladivostok from 2,400 to 1,800–2,000, and reducing the permissible number with MIRVs from 1,320 to 1,100–1,200. This option also included a range limitation of 2,500 kilometers for cruise missiles.[17] The second proposal was built on the Vladivostok levels, although reduced by ten percent, and essentially deferred resolution of the troublesome cruise missile and Backfire bomber issues.[18] A third proposal, which "essentially split the difference between the other two," was prepared to be held in reserve depending on Soviet reaction to Carter's preferred options.[19]

The first two proposals were rejected almost immediately by the Soviets, to whom Carter's reasons for deviating from the agreed framework of Vladivostok were suspect.[20] Vance cabled back for instructions on the third proposal and was informed that the president wanted him to "stand fast" on the two options presented and not raise the third.[21] Secretary Vance and Foreign Minister Gromyko then met again in Geneva for further discussions in which the U.S. proposed a "three-tier approach" that became bogged down in the details.[22]

---

[17]Zbigniew Brzezinski, *Power and Principle* (New York: Farrar, Strauss & Giroux, 1983), pp. 159-60.

[18]Carter, *Keeping Faith*, p. 219.

[19]Brzezinski. *Power and Principle*, p. 160.

[20]See, for example, Shevchenko, *Breaking with Moscow*, p. 297, wherein he states that the proposals "confused and worried Soviet rulers."

[21]Brzezinski, *Power and Principle*, p. 162.

[22]Carter, *Keeping Faith*, p. 220. As stated by President Carter: "During the two months before Vance and Gromyko met again, this time in Geneva, we developed a three-tier approach. The first agreement would be the SALT II treaty, effective through 1985; the second would last only three years and apply to a few

The president subsequently met with Gromyko in Washington on September 22, 1977, at which time the foreign minister said the Soviets were willing to proceed with the SALT II talks, but that the U.S. Senate should first ratify the Threshold Test Ban Treaty that had been signed in 1974. A few days later, on September 27, Gromyko returned to the White House along with Ambassador Dobrynin and Georgiy Kornyenko, the deputy foreign minister specializing in U.S.-Soviet relations. They were ready to agree on lower limits in strategic missiles: a ceiling of 2,250 launchers was set, 1,250 of which could be MIRVed provided that no more than 820 of these were inland-based silos.[23] It was also agreed that both sides would continue to observe the SALT I treaty (due to expire in October 1977) until the new SALT II accords could be finally agreed and implemented.

Gromyko also conveyed Brezhnev's willingness to meet at a summit provided he could be assured of its success in producing a major agreement. The Carter-Brezhnev summit was thus explicitly linked to the consummation of the SALT II treaty.

Meanwhile, the SALT negotiators in Geneva had settled into a working routine to address technical problems such as verification and the more sensitive subject, from the U.S. point of view, of encrypted telemetry in missile testing. Each side had the support of about fifteen to twenty advisers present. The U.S. team was headed by Paul Warnke until 1978, when Ralph Earle took over those responsibilities. Principal assistants included retired General George Seignious, later to become the director of the Arms Control and Disarmament Agency, and Lieutenant

---

controversial systems, such as cruise missiles and other new types; and the third would be a set of principles to guide future negotiations for a SALT III treaty involving deeper weapons reduction. Gromyko agreed to this general framework, but our two nations continued to disagree on numerous details."

[23] Ibid., p. 221.

General Edward Rowny, representing the Joint Chiefs of Staff. Vladimir Semyonov, who had headed Soviet negotiations since 1969, was chief of the Soviet delegation until replaced by Viktor Karpov, a Foreign Ministry representative with similar SALT involvement. Soviet scientist Alexander Shchukin and General Ivan Beletsky, representing the Defense Ministry, were the principal advisers.[24]

The United States SALT delegation was backed up in Washington by two specially-created organizations to oversee their progress and effect the required coordination. The National Security Council staff established a Special Coordinating Committee chaired by David Aaron, the deputy to National Security Adviser Zbigniew Brzezinski. This committee included representatives from the Defense and State Departments, the Arms Control and Disarmament Agency, and the Central Intelligence Agency. More routine problems were referred to a second body, "the SALT Backstopping Committee," chaired by Spurgeon Keeny, the deputy director of ACDA, and consisting of representatives from the same organizations as above. Considerable flexibility and overlap existed between the two groups.[25]

A number of meetings took place throughout 1978 between President Carter and Foreign Minister Gromyko, but progress on ironing out differences remaining in the SALT agreement had visibly slowed. Secretary Vance met with Gromyko in New York in May and again in Geneva in July, but no headway was made at either meeting. The president talked with Gromyko in September and conveyed his concerns about the problems associated with Soviet encryption of telemetry in their missile tests, an ongoing technical problem that inhibited U.S. efforts at verification. That meeting was more productive, and, with

---

[24]Strobe Talbott, *Endgame*, pp. 91-92.
[25]Ibid., pp. 94-95.

agreement on the fundamentals close at hand, Secretary Vance was sent to Moscow for preliminary discussions on arrangements for a summit meeting at which the final accord would be signed.

The Vance trip was unproductive, however, and the Soviets appeared reluctant to make any firm summit commitments until the remaining issues were settled.[26] One sees here the interplay of timing and circumstances in the preliminary maneuvering that precedes agreement on arrangements for a summit meeting. This was noted by President Carter, who wrote:

> With any sign of irresolution from us, the Soviets would probe for additional concessions. I told Vance to continue the discussions with Ambassador Dobrynin in Washington, maintain our basic posture on the remaining issues, and not appear too eager for a final agreement or a summit meeting. It was now obvious that although the Soviets could accept our remaining proposals, they were holding back on one or two until they could agree to the time, place, and agenda for a meeting between Brezhnev and me.[27]

Then, in December, the president announced his plan to normalize relations with China and the forthcoming visit of Deng Xiaoping to the United States in January 1979. Moscow reacted coolly to that news and made it clear that they would not discuss prospects for a summit meeting until after the Chinese leader's visit. Vance met again with Gromyko in Geneva on December 21, but the talks bogged down on finding common agreement on the definition of what constituted a "new missile."[28] Brezhnev sent Carter a letter on December 27 that showed his concern with U.S.-Chinese relations and implied that there would be no

---

[26]Carter, *Keeping Faith*, p. 233.

[27]Ibid.

[28]During this period the U.S. position was that anything more than a 5 percent change in important missile characteristics would constitute a "new missile," whereas the Soviets wanted the level set at about 20 percent change. Ibid., p. 234.

further progress on arms control unless the U.S. and its allies prevented the sale of arms to China, the prospect of which seriously concerned Soviet leaders.

Early in January 1979 President Carter met in Guadeloupe with French President Valéry Giscard d'Estaing, British Prime Minister James Callaghan and German Chancellor Helmut Schmidt for a review of relations with the Soviets. Their talks focused on the threats posed by Soviet deployment of the intermediate-range SS-20 missile against Western Europe and what the appropriate response should be. As later recounted by Carter:

> The conversation was obviously inconclusive, but typical of the problem the United States had faced for a long time in shaping a response to Soviet threats against Europe. I was prepared to negotiate with Brezhnev about an overall reduction in these armaments; but, pending an agreement, Europe had to be willing to maintain the strength of our joint forces so that they would at least be competitive with those of the Soviet Union. The European leaders would let the United States design, develop, and produce the new weapons, but none of them was willing to agree in advance to deploy them.[29]

Following the Chinese Vice Premier's visit, U.S.-Soviet relations were temporarily set back when the Chinese crossed the North Vietnamese border in February for a retaliatory attack. President Carter rejected Soviet charges of complicity in the incident and summoned Ambassador Dobrynin to the White House to stress the need for corrective action to prevent further deterioration in their relations.

Then, on March 2, Brezhnev spoke out in favor of the SALT agreements and accepted the U.S. position to prohibit encryption and limit "new" missile modifications.[30] On April 7 Secretary Vance advised the president

---

[29]Ibid., p. 235.
[30]The Soviets accepted the U.S. definition of 5 percent change as a limit. Ibid., p. 238.

that Brezhnev was ready to conclude the SALT agreement and wanted an early summit.

The state of Brezhnev's health was a serious consideration in making arrangements for the summit meeting. Vienna was quickly agreed upon as its desired location, and the Soviets made it clear that they wanted "no surprises" at the summit, with direct consultations limited to a relatively brief duration.[31] According to one observer, the Soviets were concerned about whether President Carter could deliver on the ratification of the SALT agreement, and this was another reason that Vienna was selected as the conference site:

> The Soviets saw that risk clearly as they prepared for the summit, and possibly one reason they contrived to hold the meeting on neutral ground—quite aside from minimizing the strain on Brezhnev's shaky health—was to avoid the additional political hazard of sending their leader all the way to the U.S. to sign a document that might end up on the trash heap of history.[32]

The setting of June 15 as the convening date for the summit put additional pressures on the SALT negotiators to resolve their remaining disagreements on technical issues. Most of these were relatively minor, although the matter of who should make the final concession on sticking points assumed a symbolic importance out of proportion to their strategic significance. The full delegations convened twenty times in the last ten days of negotiations, and the documents that Carter and Brezhnev would eventually sign in Vienna were still not completed by the time the president departed Washington on June 14 for the summit.[33]

Internal preparations were extensive. The president demanded and received detailed position papers from

---

[31] Zbigniew Brzezinski, *Power and Principle*, p. 340.
[32] Talbott, *Endgame*, p. 12.
[33] Ibid., p. 7.

every concerned government department and agency. As described in Strobe Talbott's account of SALT II:

> Carter's appetite for homework seemed insatiable. He kept calling for more papers, more briefings—on the background and ramifications of any subject that might conceivably come up at the summit. He had always tended to immerse himself in the detail of any task. He had a compulsive desire—and, indeed, a prodigious ability—to master the most technical aspects of his job. Even some of his most loyal supporters and assistants felt that in this respect he was conscientious to a fault, that he wasted time and energy on minutiae, that there was an obsessive quality to his meticulousness. It was as though he thought he could beat any problem simply by understanding it to death. But in this case, there may well have been an extra—and uncharacteristic—element of apprehension, even insecurity, in his over-preparation. The talks with Brezhnev . . . promised to be a critical test of Carter's much-criticized competence as president.[34]

In a comprehensive memorandum for the president, Brzezinski noted his concerns with the Soviet military buildup and increased activity in the Indian Ocean area and urged the president to go beyond the SALT agreement and seek a broader dialogue on how these matters had a negative impact on the American public and thus on détente.[35] On June 8 Secretary Vance stressed to Carter that "the primary focus of your exchanges with Brezhnev should be to reaffirm the basic framework of U.S.-Soviet relations, which is based on substantial common interest in strategic stability, mutual acceptance of the status quo in the developed world and avoidance of confrontation in dealing with the Third World."[36]

The president took these and a substantial number of briefing books compiled by the National Security Council

---

[34]Ibid., pp. 2-3.

[35]Brzezinksi, *Power and Principle*, p. 340.

[36]Quoted in ibid.

staff to Camp David for further study on his last weekend in Washington before the summit meeting. Prior to his departure he also had a long talk with former Ambassador Averell Harriman on what to expect from the Soviet leader at Vienna. In his departure remarks on June 14, President Carter stated his purposes:

> I approach this summit in Vienna with hope, but without any false expectations. The goals which lie at the heart of my mission today—improving our own nation's security and enhancing the prospects for world peace and the avoidance of nuclear war—transcend all other issues that I will ever face in my own life in public service.[37]

Accompanying the president were Secretary of State Vance; Secretary of Defense Harold Brown; National Security Adviser Brzezinski; General David Jones, Chairman of the Joint Chiefs of Staff; ACDA Director George Seignious; Ralph Earle, chief of the U.S. delegation at the SALT negotiations; Ambassador Malcolm Toon; and Presidential Assistants Hamilton Jordan and Jody Powell.[38] Their Soviet counterparts, joining General Secretary Brezhnev and Foreign Minister Gromyko, consisted of Minister of Defense Dmitriy Ustinov and his first deputy (and chief of the General Staff of the Armed Forces), Marshal Nikolai Ogarkov; Secretary of the Central Committee of the CPSU Konstantin Chernenko; the chief of the Soviet delegation at the SALT negotiations, Viktor Karpov; Ambassador Dobrynin; and the assistant to the general secretary, Andrei Aleksandrov.

Upon their arrival on June 14, the two leaders first met at the Austrian presidential palace for a formal call on

---

[37]U.S. Department of State, Bureau of Public Affairs, *Selected Documents No. 13: Vienna Summit*, p. 1.
[38]Lieutenant General Rowny "respectfully declined" to attend the signing ceremony as a gesture of protest against the "unwarranted and dangerous concessions" made by the United States in the negotiations, according to Talbott in *Endgame*, p. 6.

President Rudolf Kirchschlaeger and Chancellor Bruno
Kreisky. This was followed by a very brief meeting of the
two leaders that generally focused on pleasantries and
attendance at the evening's opera. They began their formal
meetings the next day at the U.S. Embassy, since it was
America's turn to host the conference. General Secretary
Brezhnev stated that the major result of the summit would
be the SALT II agreement, but he did not exclude the
importance of discussing other problems, notably including the arms race in general and increased U.S. defense
spending in particular. President Carter then countered
and observed the substantial budget increases for the
Soviets' own military buildup over the course of the last
fifteen years and stated that this effort was hardly matched
by U.S. spending.[39]

The afternoon session on June 15 was devoted to the
SALT II agreement. As part of the prearrangements, both
sides were required to read into the record certain statements concerning their understandings. On the U.S. side
these consisted of statements on the cruise missiles and
Minuteman missiles, and on the Soviet side a statement
regarding limitation on production of the Backfire bomber
to no more than thirty a year. But Brezhnev failed to follow
the carefully crafted script on the latter point and only
made an evasive comment about it. Both leaders then
exchanged statements expressing agreement that there
would be no encoding of missile test data covered by the
items in the SALT II treaty that would interfere with the
other side's verification measures. On the next day, President Carter told Brezhnev that his statement on limiting
the Backfire production rate had been equivocal and that it
had been agreed previously he would explicitly state their
limitation to be thirty a year. After a lengthy altercation on

---

[39]Carter, *Keeping Faith*, p. 249.

the negotiating history of that subject, the general secretary finally came forth with the pre-scripted response.

Other discussions focused on prospects for a SALT III agreement, nonproliferation of nuclear weapons, and various trouble spots around the world. At Brezhnev's request on June 17, President Carter provided him with a handwritten list of proposals he had made concerning SALT III, which included, among the dozen items, a commitment to "deep cuts" in the SALT II limits, a cessation of nuclear warhead and launcher production, a comprehensive test ban treaty, and agreement not to undertake testing of anti-satellite systems.[40]

Before signing the SALT II treaty on the last day of the summit, June 18, the two sides continued discussions on matters of mutual concern—for the U.S., most notably the human rights issue, and for the Soviets, the U.S.-Chinese rapprochement. Brezhnev rejected the former as inappropriate subject matter for bilateral talks and returned to his concern about China. President Carter assured the Soviet leader that the new U.S. relationship with China would not be used to the detriment of the Soviet Union.[41]

The president and the general secretary then signed the SALT II agreements that formally consisted of the Treaty on Limitation of Strategic Offensive Arms, along with Agreed Statements and Common Understandings thereto, its Protocol, and the Joint Statement of Principles and Basic Guidelines for Subsequent Negotiations on the Limitation of Strategic Arms. Additionally, Ambassador Earle and Viktor Karpov, chiefs of their respective SALT negotiating delegations, signed a Memorandum of Understanding Regarding the Establishment of a Data Base on the Numbers of Strategic Offensive Arms, along with a

---

[40]The complete list is reproduced in ibid., p. 253.
[41]Ibid., p. 259.

Statement of Data that stipulated the agreed numbers for each side.

The joint communiqué had been drafted before the summit commenced. This is the usual practice, as described by Garthoff:

> Diplomatic communiqués purporting to summarize and report on conferences reflect the actual proceedings only in part. Not only are some things suppressed or glossed over, but many—and sometimes important—statements in communiqués may never have been mentioned in the meeting of the principals. Moreover, the language of communiqués is often drafted and negotiated, and occasionally completed, before the meetings begin. The actual hammering out of language by their representatives does not merely record agreements, but is the forum that determines the areas of agreement. The communiqué on the Vienna meeting was mainly drafted in Washington beforehand by senior representatives of the Department of State and the Soviet embassy. The Soviet representatives consulted with Moscow for instructions and approval on a number of occasions during the preparation of the text.[42]

The Vienna communiqué noted mutual intentions to seek progress on a comprehensive test ban treaty, mutual and balanced force reductions in Europe, limitation of conventional arms transfers as well as strict compliance on nuclear nonproliferation, and movement toward the prohibition of chemical weapons and radiological weapons. Statements on international issues included support for the Final Act of the Conference on Security and Cooperation in Europe, signed in Helsinki in 1975; for the All-European Conference, scheduled to convene in Madrid in 1980; and for bilateral meetings on arms limitation measures in the Indian Ocean area. The communiqué also stated:

---

[42]Garthoff, *Détente and Confrontation*, pp. 735-36.

The talks again confirmed the specific significance of personal meetings between the leaders of the USA and the USSR in resolving the basic questions in the relations between the two states. In principle, it has been agreed that such meetings will be held in the future on a regular basis, with the understanding that specific timing will be determined by mutual agreement.[43]

Upon President Carter's return to Washington on June 18 he addressed the Congress and hailed the SALT II accords as "the most detailed, far-reaching, comprehensive treaty in the history of arms control."[44] He sent the treaty to the Senate on June 22 for ratification, but that was not to be. Notwithstanding the growing objections of conservatives, which made the prospects for ratification questionable, it was the Soviet invasion of Afghanistan in December of the same year that effectively precluded any further hopes for Senate endorsement of the treaty. As observed by the president in his memoirs: "Our failure to ratify the SALT II treaty and to secure even more far-reaching agreements on nuclear arms control was the most profound disappointment of my Presidency. However, with the antagonism that Soviet action in Afghanistan had kindled in our country, ratification was, for the time being, an impossible task."[45]

---

[43]Joint U.S.-U.S.S.R. Communiqué" issued at Vienna on June 18, 1979 and reproduced in *Selected Documents No. 13*, op. cit., p. 7.

[44]President Carter's Address to Congress, June 18, 1979, ibid., p. 9.

[45]Carter, *Keeping Faith*, p. 265.

6

Conclusions

THE RECORD OF the ten U.S.-Soviet summits from 1955 to 1979 is marked by the irregularity of their occurrence, the mixed motivations and rationale prompting them, the varying nature of their conduct and results and, certainly, the changing international and domestic contexts in which they have taken place since 1955. As observed in the quotation by President Eisenhower at the outset of this review, generalizations about summitry are to be considered suspect because of the great differences in circumstance that surround such meetings of heads of state. But the foregoing narrative does suggest that some observations can be offered with regard to the elements of the processes involved that may serve to summarize the findings of this study. First, however, it may be useful to step back for a moment and consider some broader aspects of the record.

To begin, the composition of the summits has changed from the multilateral East-West configuration in the Eisenhower years to the subsequent bilateral U.S.-Soviet approach. The 1955 Geneva Conference of Heads of Government was patterned after the type used by the wartime allies at Tehran, Yalta and Potsdam, except that the Cold War had now split their unity. And even though

Khrushchev's visit to the United States in 1959 involved discussions with only one Western leader—a president who viewed the meetings as preliminary to a summit at most— Eisenhower was careful to coordinate fully with his British and French counterparts, as well as with Chancellor Adenauer, before the talks commenced. The ill-fated Paris summit of the following year marked the last attempt by the Western allies to meet together at the summit with Soviet leaders.

Second, it is also apparent that there has been a clear shift in summit rationale from the earlier emphasis on international tensions to the later focus on strategic arms limitation between the superpowers. Eisenhower's objective at Geneva was "to define crucial world issues" for subsequent negotiation and, it was hoped, resolution by the foreign ministers of the four powers. The common thread of problems stemming from the German reunification issue and Soviet threats on Berlin persisted through President Kennedy's meeting with Khrushchev in Vienna. But at the next summit, the 1967 Glassboro talks between President Johnson and Premier Kosygin, a significant shift to strategic weapons began and has since become the centerpiece of U.S.-Soviet summits. To say this is not to deny summit discussions about international crises their position of importance in the more recent meetings—surely the Vietnam War, Middle East eruptions, and the emergence of improved U.S.-Chinese relations provided the overall context in which the summits were set—but only to point out the now-central position of strategic arms limitations in the summit agenda.

Third, and perhaps as a corollary of this shift in emphasis, the trend has been from general discussions to specific and signed agreements, most notably as begun in the Nixon-Brezhnev summit of 1972 and continued since. Whereas the earlier summits tended to consolidate results in lofty objectives enunciated in communiqués, the later ones produced formal agreements, highly technical in the case of those related to SALT and quite specific in the case of those relating to cooperative efforts. The shift from a summit "spirit" to achievement of concrete results has become the accepted criterion of success.

A fourth observation that can be made concerns the irregular pattern of summit timing. Except for the reciprocating nature of the Nixon-Brezhnev summits, the summits have occurred with seemingly haphazard frequency. The six-year interval between the Kennedy-Khrushchev summit in Vienna in 1961 and the rather "spur-of-the-moment" Glassboro meeting in 1967 was followed by a five-year interval before the start of annual summits in the Nixon-Brezhnev years. Then, after the Vladivostok talks between Ford and Brezhnev in 1974, there ensued another lengthy interval, only to be exceeded in duration by the period following the Carter-Brezhnev meeting in Vienna in 1979.

Fifth, the locations for nine of the ten summits have been evenly distributed with three each on U.S. territory (Khrushchev's visit in 1959, the Glassboro talks in 1967, and Brezhnev's visit in 1973); on Soviet territory (the 1972 and 1974 Moscow summits, and 1974 Vladivostok talks); and in "neutral" locations (Geneva in 1955, and Vienna in 1961 and 1979), with the other being the aborted Paris summit in 1960. With that record established, there appears nothing exceptional about the "neutral" location of the Reagan-Gorbachev November 1985 summit in Geneva. In terms of their sequence and sense of protocol, it may be noted that the two summits before the last both occurred on Soviet soil, but Moscow could easily point out that none of the first five summits took place there.

A sixth and final general observation drawn from the summit record is that whereas six American presidents have participated in such meetings, Soviet representation has been primarily limited to two leaders—Khrushchev attended four, Brezhnev five, and Kosygin only one as the principal. Whatever conclusions may follow from this in terms of negotiating experience at such meetings are at best tentative. The comparison becomes more marked when one recalls that Gromyko participated in all ten summits and that there has been a remarkable consistency in Soviet personnel on the SALT negotiations.

To the above observations it may also be relevant to add that the differences in political and social systems between the two countries tend to produce a number of other asymmetries in the summit process that are both visible and of significance to the conduct and results of the meetings, but observations here may exceed the scope of the present inquiry. The most important of these relate to the degree and scope of control exercised by the two leaders over their respective countries: at the 1979 Vienna summit, for example, Brezhnev did not really have to worry that once he signed the SALT II treaty it might later be rejected in Moscow, as was its fate in Washington.[1] The cycle of presidential elections, the role of a free press, pressures of public expectations, among numerous other domestic considerations of great difference in the two countries, surely affect their leaders' orientation, motivation and flexibility at the summit conference table.

The Preparation Process in Review

RETURNING NOW TO some elements of the summit preparation process, it is clear, first, that the timing of a summit initiative has been a critical factor in gauging the

---

[1]As noted by Talbott in *Endgame*, p. 15: "At the summit, Brezhnev made clear he was aware of, and not unsympathetic toward, Carter's political problems over SALT. 'Your system is somewhat different than ours,' said the Soviet leader privately. 'We really don't have much doubt about the ratification process in our country.'"

prospects for successful encounters. Perhaps the best example of this is the shrewdness with which Richard Nixon and Henry Kissinger managed to coordinate the date of the 1972 Moscow summit with the completion of the SALT I accords, the U.S. opening with China, and events in the Vietnam War. Because of U.S. initiatives in all three areas, the relaxation of tensions between Washington and Moscow—détente—became a matter of common interest and mutual benefit to both countries at that time. Beyond the concerns of both about avoiding nuclear confrontation, the U.S. had developed a sophisticated strategy to make it in Moscow's interest to help extricate America from involvement in Vietnam, and the Soviet Union had new concerns with China that made better relations with the United States more important to them. That commonality of interest provided the circumstances for the opportune timing of the summit, as well as for the substantive results achieved.

On the other side of this coin, poor timing and inopportune circumstances were reflected in the Kennedy-Khrushchev summit at Vienna in 1961. Not only did this follow the aborted Paris summit of the previous year, but the contentious issue of Berlin remained the major issue of disagreement during the interval. If it was indeed the problem of Berlin that was at the root of the Paris failure (and not the pretext of the U-2 incident), and if that problem remained unsolved, it is difficult to see how the Vienna summit could turn out much better than its predecessor. Moreover, Khrushchev's need for a foreign policy success was coupled with Kennedy's poor showing the previous April with the Bay of Pigs fiasco. Given the lingering Berlin problem, a Soviet leader pressed to show success, and an apparently inexperienced U.S. president, it may not, in retrospect, be surprising that the summit produced little more than a renewal of Soviet threats against Berlin.

Beyond these two examples, which are relatively clear-cut, the relation of timing and circumstance to summit success becomes less evident and more submerged in the ebb and flow of U.S.-Soviet relations. The Geneva summit in 1955 arose out of the Cold War period after the end of the Korean War, when both East and West were looking for some means of relaxing mutual suspicions and tensions. In this sense, its timing may have been opportune, but circumstances were still only marginally conducive to reaching any significant breakthroughs (the Quemoy-Matsu crisis was contemporaneous with that summit). Neither side, particularly Eisenhower and Dulles, had any great expectations about the summit, and the president's evaluation of it as a "limited success" was entirely apt. His 1959 meeting with Khrushchev was timely in averting a possible confrontation on the Berlin problem, but that situation remained unresolved and significantly affected the following two summits, as stated above.

President Johnson's meeting at Glassboro with Premier Kosygin in 1967 was so hastily arranged that significant results could hardly be expected. The Soviet premier was a reluctant participant and most likely not authorized to get involved in the discussions sought by Johnson and McNamara on anti-ballistic missile systems. Soviet concerns at the time focused on getting the U.S. to pressure Israel to withdraw from lands occupied in the Six-Day War and to withdraw its own forces from Vietnam. The crossed purposes and short lead time to prepare for the summit produced "next to nothing," as Kosygin put it at the time. That meeting, however, led to U.S.-Soviet co-sponsorship in 1968 of the U.N. resolution that resulted in the treaty on nuclear nonproliferation, which was signed by the two superpowers (and 60 other countries) on July 1 of that year. The Glassboro meeting, moreover, planted the seed that eventually led to the 1972 ABM Treaty.

By the time of Brezhnev's visit to the United States in 1973, U.S. involvement in Vietnam was being wound down based on the Paris Agreements of the preceding January, and different motivations attended President Nixon's approach to the Soviet leader than had been the case a year earlier in Moscow. As recounted by Kissinger, the U.S. was able to stall on Moscow's "nuclear condominium" gambit and finally got Brezhnev to accept a watered-down version of his original goals in the Agreement on the Prevention of Nuclear War. As at all three Nixon-Brezhnev summits, a host of cooperative agreements were signed, but the backwash of anti-détente sentiment in the United States and the ever-closing net of the Watergate investigations combined to make substantive progress on strategic offensive missile limitations out of reach. President Ford's meeting at Vladivostok with Brezhnev in November 1974, which succeeded in reaching agreement on the framework for limitation of those missiles, was a notable achievement in the midst of the turmoil created by Nixon's resignation in August. Regardless of its technical merits or deficiencies, the Vladivostok summit provided a restored sense of continuity to the SALT process.

The achievement of SALT II accords at Vienna in 1979 has been observed as a somewhat anomalous event. Détente had waned, and conservative reaction to U.S. failure in Vietnam, Soviet aggression in Angola via Cuban proxies, and the overall status of U.S. military strength vis-a-vis the continued Soviet buildup all combined to make further agreement with the Soviets unpalatable to a growing number of Americans. The fall of the shah of Iran in early 1979 added to perceptions of U.S. weakness (more dramatically projected later in November when U.S. embassy personnel were taken hostage in Tehran) and made the meeting between Carter and Brezhnev in June seem out of context. The Senate's failure to ratify the treaty promptly reflected as much a concern with its timing and international context as it did the debate on its merits. The Soviet invasion of Afghanistan in December of that year sealed its fate, as well as setting the stage against any further summit initiatives until the Reagan-Gorbachev maneuvering began in March 1985.

From what has been presented in the survey of these summits it does not appear that the determination of conference location has been a major factor in the process. As stated above, their distribution between U.S., Soviet and "neutral" sites has been fairly even. Only at the 1967 Glassboro meeting did the issue of conference site become an evident problem; but that summit had an exceptionally short lead time. It may well be that Kosygin used the location issue as a pretext to avoid meeting with President Johnson, as Shevchenko has speculated. The selection of Vienna in 1979 has already been commented on as most likely chosen for reasons of Brezhnev's health.

The way in which the Reagan-Gorbachev arrangements evolved, however, suggests that there was a certain degree of sensitivity about the location of this summit. It appears that the president clearly wanted the meeting in Washington and felt that protocol supported that choice. With Gorbachev demurring, he reportedly offered to go to Moscow for a second summit if the new Soviet leader came to Washington first, but this offer did not work either. Their agreement to meet in Geneva took almost four months to reach. This may not be unusual in terms of the time required for the new leader to establish himself and his plans, but was quite possibly an uncomfortable delay for the president, who initiated the summit proposal and whose prestige was on the line.

The use of formal "preconditions" for summit meetings with the Soviets was most pronounced under Eisenhower, whose insistence on preconditions precluded the advent of the first postwar summit for a year or two beyond the desires of his British and French counterparts. By the time of the 1955 Geneva Heads of Government Conference, the foreign ministers had met several times to prepare for the summit and there were reasonable prospects for a productive meeting, although full agreement on the agenda had not been possible. Eisenhower repeatedly insisted on fulfillment of the preconditions before agreeing to meet with Khrushchev in 1959, an event that he did not consider a summit meeting but rather a "pre-summit." President Nixon's determined efforts to get Moscow to help end the Vietnam war prior to the 1972 summit constituted the next example of a precondition. No similar application of preconditions to subsequent summits was evident until President Reagan, in his first term, established his own set of requirements for consideration of summit prospects. Their apparent deletion from his invitation to Gorbachev may thus be seen in part as a measure of his increased willingness to meet the new leader on an equal footing.

The process of arriving at an agreed-upon agenda has generally followed determination of the date and location of such meetings. As observed earlier, this appears to be a practical necessity for administrative and logistical matters. Eisenhower's determination to achieve agreement on an agenda before agreeing to summit meetings was only partially successful. The agenda was not entirely fixed before the start of the 1955 Geneva summit, thus necessitating additional work on it by the foreign ministers after the conference had started. In 1959, Secretary Herter and Foreign Minister Gromyko worked out agreement on an agenda the day after Khrushchev arrived for his visit to the United States, and it was not rigidly adhered to by the leaders at Camp David. And despite intensive coordination among the allies on the agenda for the 1960 Paris summit, their efforts were moot in light of the summit's failure following the U-2 incident.

President Kennedy's meeting with Khrushchev the

following year in Vienna was less structured and more freely ranging—the former talked about accommodation and avoidance of conflict in nonvital areas, whereas the latter expounded upon peaceful coexistence and wars of national liberation. In terms of ideology they were at cross-purposes, and the meeting produced agreement only on mutual restraint in Laos. The Johnson-Kosygin talks in Glassboro in 1967 were arranged on such short notice that agreement on an agenda was not possible. Again, the leaders were at cross-purposes.

The Nixon-Brezhnev summits were almost entirely arranged and pre-scripted by Henry Kissinger's coordination in Washington with Ambassador Dobrynin and his advance trips to Moscow for direct consultations with Brezhnev and Gromyko. He orchestrated the preparation of the numerous treaties and agreements to be signed at the summits, the communiqués and announcements, and the agenda details, so that Nixon and Brezhnev could walk into their meetings with visible assurances of success. Beyond negotiating on the final sticking points of the SALT I treaty at the 1972 Moscow summit, the leaders were relatively free to focus on their differences in more candid discussions out of the public limelight, where disagreements could be kept private and shrouded under the aura of "pre-cooked" successes. As recounted by participants, the more sensitive issues generally included Vietnam, the Middle East, and Moscow's increasing concerns about China. In view of the president's imperiled position due to Watergate, the 1974 Moscow summit was so tightly crafted that the president was even freer than before to pursue serious discussions on international problems. In that sense, Kissinger felt it was successful, despite the fact that agreement on limitation of strategic offensive missiles was not in the offing.

In similar fashion, Kissinger prearranged Gerald Ford's

meeting with Brezhnev at Vladivostok. During his October trip to Moscow, an agenda was set calling for discussions on SALT the first day and international problems the second. President Ford stated after the summit, in his news conference of December 2, 1974, that he and Brezhnev had been able to agree in principle on the upper limits of strategic offensive missiles, thus providing the framework for subsequent negotiations culminating in the SALT II treaty.

The 1979 Vienna summit agenda was built around the signing of that treaty. Advance arrangements specifically limited the scope and duration of discussions on other subjects out of consideration for Brezhnev's health. The more formal aspects of the summit regarding the SALT II treaty were entirely prescripted, as evidenced by Brezhnev's initial misstep on the mandatory Backfire statement and Carter's later insistence upon it in accordance with prior agreement on that matter.

Strict focus on the formal agenda and substantive outcomes tends to obscure the value of the face-to-face contacts favorably noted by every president involved in the postwar summit experience with the Soviets. In particular, President Eisenhower found his informal discussions with Soviet leaders at Geneva far more useful than the rigid formality observed in the plenary sessions. President Kennedy's purpose at Vienna was specifically geared to the conduct of such discussions with Khrushchev and not the accumulation of signed agreements. The same held true for President Johnson at Glassboro. Moreover, despite President Nixon's emphasis on concrete results and the flurry of signed agreements, both he and Kissinger have stated that the informal meetings constituted the best use of the leaders' time at the summits. The importance of that contact was specifically cited in the communiqué released after the Vienna summit of 1979. In light of these observations, it would seem that some reevaluation of the purposes best served by summit meetings may be in order, particularly so with regard to public expectations and intense media attention, which tend to pressure presidents into signing documents as "proof" of success, instead of concentrating on the less sensational—but more meaningful— conduct of discussion.

One final observation that should be addressed concerns the precept that in order to succeed a summit must be well-prepared. In a sense this is as self-evident as it is ambiguous. There is clearly no dispute that summits are deadly serious occasions and every possible detail should be arranged with great care and forethought to preclude inadvertent mishaps from affecting the proceedings. The administrative and logistical preparations made by the advance teams are complicated and essential to a smooth-running summit. These include the behind-the-scenes arrangements for security, communications, media coordination, accommodations, social functions and protocol matters, any one of which could have an adverse impact on the proceedings if not properly attended to at the outset.

Important as such matters are in establishing the physical and mechanical foundations for the summit meetings, however, even more critical to success at the summit are the substantive preparations geared to the objectives of the particular summit. Variance in summit objectives—from the conduct of discussions only through a spectrum of discussions and signed agreements—implies differing criteria for what is considered success, and preparations must vary accordingly. If the president decides that signed agreements are his goal, then adequate preparations focus on finding areas of agreement between the United States and the Soviet Union that can be reduced to written documents to be signed by the leaders. This is precisely what was done in the three Nixon summits: agreements were searched out by Kissinger, drafted in final form, and held ready for signature at the summit.

This type of substantive preparation produced the desired success, but not just because preparations matched goals; both the U.S. and the Soviet Union had determined that détente was in their best interests, albeit for different reasons. In short, then, the president's definition of success at the summit was achieved, with the aid of proper preparation, because it was in the national interest of both countries to conclude the proposed agreements.

Therefore, it would appear that "adequate preparations" for a summit meeting start with a clear definition of the intended goals, which can then be translated into appropriately matched efforts. However, the desired ends can be achieved only when the state of U.S.-Soviet relations is conducive to producing agreement and when mutual benefit is possible. The effectiveness of preparations, in and of themselves, however skillfully carried out, remains subject to the international context in which the summit is held. That context can not be manipulated with such facility as to produce success when international realities indicate otherwise. An accurate appraisal of those realities is the craft of successful statesmen in the conduct of summit diplomacy.

Epilogue:
Back to Square One

Dusko Doder

SUMMIT MEETINGS BETWEEN leaders of the United States and the Soviet Union have become an essential feature of modern times. Some attribute this, in part, to the emergence of an increasingly complex and basically unmanageable world with a multitude of new states. Others blame it, more specifically, on technology; nuclear weapons have made it suicidal to try to settle quarrels between the two superpowers by reaching for the ultimate means.

A combination of these strategic circumstances produced the November 1985 summit between President Reagan and Soviet leader Mikhail Gorbachev. The Geneva meeting was the outcome of widely different tactics pursued by the two sides following the collapse of Soviet-American détente in the early eighties. For the collapse of détente itself had produced a new situation which became envenomed by neglect, inflamed alike by the "evil empire" rhetoric and the poison of Tass retorts. In 1983 and the beginning of 1984 thoughtful persons on both sides feared the possibility of an inadvertent slide down the slippery slope of passion, propaganda gestures and threats to a more treacherous position from which retreats would be difficult. The Soviet walkout from the Geneva arms talks in late 1983 signified an overall breakdown in Soviet-American relations, a breakoff of substantive contacts; diplomacy, for both sides, became an exercise in public relations. The situation was unacceptably dangerous.

The downward slide had started in early 1980, shortly after the Soviet invasion of Afghanistan, which had led to a series of U.S. punitive measures against Moscow—a grain embargo, a ban on the sale of high technology, restrictions on Soviet fishing in U.S. waters, withdrawal from the 1980 Moscow Olympics and a series of other steps. Reagan in his 1980 campaign speeches advocated halting all trade with the Soviet Union, a moratorium on all treaties with Moscow, and other Soviet-bashing schemes. By the time of the 1985 summit, the Russians were still in Afghanistan and American grain was flowing freely to Russia.

So, what had led Reagan to advance the idea of meeting with Gorbachev a few days after the latter became general secretary of the Soviet Communist Party? What did their meeting in Geneva accomplish?

No doubt Reagan and his advisers were curious about the young new Soviet leader and eager to take his measure. No doubt, too, the protracted Kremlin power transition had left the Americans with an impression of the passing of the Kremlin's authority into the hands of a largely unknown and possibly inexperienced man who might lack the toughness of his old guard predecessors. If this were so, Reagan and his advisers could press Gorbachev in direct encounter to accept Reagan's concept of superpowers' dialogue. Moreover, by making his invitation public, Reagan would put Gorbachev in a position where he could not turn it down without appearing unnecessarily unyielding and hostile. A Gorbachev rejection would weaken Moscow's international position since the hope of arms limitation meant a great deal to the rest of the world; apart from their desire to regulate their strategic relationship with the United States, the Russians had used arms control to present themselves as humankind's party of hope and nuclear responsibility.

Such motives could explain the timing of Reagan's decision to extend the invitation hours after Gorbachev's predecessor, Konstantin Chernenko, was buried behind the Lenin Mausoleum. Given his age, Gorbachev could live long enough to deal with a series of American presidents for the rest of this century.

But summitry is part of a fluid process that regulates relations between the two nuclear superpowers, both obsessed with their rivalry yet both condemned to keep that contest within manageable limits to avoid a nuclear war.

If the Russians entertained hopes that they could manage to salvage the arms control process, those hopes were badly shaken on March 23, 1983, when Reagan unveiled his Strategic Defense Initiative. From that point on, public temper had been gradually mounting, octave by octave, and it was obvious that the need to counteract the deployment of new American nuclear missiles in Europe would soon be forcing active decisions on the Andropov government. The shooting down of a civilian Korean Airlines plane by a Soviet jet fighter on September 1, 1983 sealed the confrontational mode. It was the sort of situation in which leaders could not ignore the possibility of war by accident or miscalculation.

In January 1984, Reagan began to signal a change in attitude by moderating his rhetoric in a speech on the need for "peaceful competition" between the two superpowers and their "common interest" in avoiding war. His pre-conditions for a serious dialogue with the Russians had been met; he had revived the American economy while mounting a huge rearmament program, launched his Star Wars plan, and deployed new Pershing II and cruise missiles in Western Europe. He was, at the same time, under pressure from America's allies and American public opinion to restore the dialogue with Moscow. The emergence of a mass antiwar movement in an election year was a problem that had to be defused.

Moscow's response to Reagan's signal was harsh. Both publicly and privately, Yuri Andropov, the Soviet leader at the time, made it clear that the resumption of dialogue would have to be on Soviet terms. These included a demand for the removal of Pershing II and cruise missiles from Western Europe—an impossible request since Reagan and other NATO leaders had spent considerable political capital to carry out the deployment plan. Moreover, Andropov questioned the very policy of détente with the United States, which had become personally identified with his predecessor, Leonid Brezhnev. At the time of Brezhnev's death in 1982, Moscow's relations with the United States had moved in an almost complete circle—from Cold War hostilities to détente and back again. From Moscow's perspective, what Brezhnev thought of as an irreversible process had in fact been reversed by the Reagan administration. Andropov, in September of 1983, publicly suggested that détente with America, while desirable, was no longer possible.

Despite forebodings about a gloom-laden 1984, Andropov's death in February changed the atmosphere. The Kremlin transition itself seemed to offer an opportunity to arrest the downward slide in relations between Moscow and Washington. These relations had deteriorated to a point at which a fresh start toward improvement would require a summit meeting. Western editorialists and some Western statesmen raised the possibility of a summit. Moreover, the new Soviet leader, Konstantin Chernenko, moved quickly to moderate Moscow's policy; the portents of the day became less disquieting and the mechanisms of the government shifted toward accommodation.

It was in the summer of 1984 that Chernenko reached two critical decisions that opened the way for the resumption of dialogue and the eventual Geneva summit. The key decision was Moscow's conviction that Reagan would be reelected in November. From this flowed the second—and for the Russians even more unpalatable—decision, to abandon Andropov's insistence on the removal of Pershing II and cruise missiles from Europe.

From that point onward, the Russians began signaling their desire to move toward accommodation, or at least to avoid a full-blown revival of the cold war. Among a variety of signals from both capitals the most important was the decision for Soviet Foreign Minister Andrei Gromyko to meet President Reagan in September of 1984.

The possibility of a summit meeting had been discussed during Chernenko's tenure. But Reagan had one more precondition; he insisted on the resumption of arms talks. After Chernenko signaled that the removal of Pershing II and cruise missiles was no longer a precondition, the two sides announced that Secretary of State George P. Shultz and Gromyko would meet in Geneva in January of 1985 to work out a framework for new arms talks. The way for a summit meeting was now clear; the mechanics of the process now became its substance.

In January, however, Chernenko's health deteriorated sharply and he vanished from public view. The discussions conducted through diplomatic channels continued but without energy and enthusiasm from Moscow. Chernenko died two days before the opening of the Geneva talks on strategic, medium-range and space weapons.

Reagan's prompt invitation to Gorbachev—while reflecting the previous talks about the possibility of a summit—gave the process a public dimension. The American president seized the initiative; he also invited Gorbachev to come to Washington. Gorbachev's advisers promptly ruled out a visit to Washington; they suspected that the Americans were trying to have a Kennedy-Khrushchev meeting in reverse, an older man curious

about his untested young adversary. They saw Reagan's
invitation as a ploy to impress Gorbachev with the
achievements of American technology and industry and
thus put him on the defensive. But the publicly announced
invitation could not be turned down by the new leader. So
Moscow accepted the summit proposal in principle, and
the process came down to determining the date and
place.

It should not require a great leap of imagination to grasp
that Soviet politicians, like those in the United States, play
roles that are larger than life and not entirely their own;
that, like their Western counterparts, they are interested in
enhancing their image with an eye on History; that they
resort to tidy and not so tidy expediencies to reconcile
various pressure groups and interests; and that, without a
doubt, somewhere in the back of their minds, they believe
they are helping to improve the world, or at least their
country's lot in it. It is difficult to establish with any
precision what Gorbachev's motives were for accepting
Reagan's proposal. Even the signals seemed far too elusive
for the exactness of scholarship. The decision taken so
early into Gorbachev's tenure must have been a collective
one, however. For it seemed at the time that the Russians
were accepting Reagan's idea of a "get-acquainted
summit," something they had derided in the past.

Two elements served as powerful incentives for the new
Soviet leader and his advisors to go to the summit. One, it
was likely to strengthen Gorbachev's position both at home
and abroad; and two, it would provide him with the
opportunity personally to assess Reagan's intentions on
arms control. The latter point was of practical urgency
since the Kremlin was preparing its economic plans for the
rest of the decade.

Negotiations about the place and date were conducted
through Anatoliy Dobrynin, the Soviet ambassador in
Washington, and American Ambassador Arthur Hartman

in Moscow. By July, when the two sides reached agreement to hold the meeting in Geneva on November 19–21, virtually no preparations had been made on the substantive aspect of the summit. For the subsequent four months, the process of negotiating technical aspects of the summit was in the hands of middle-level officials who included, on the American side, Assistant Secretary of State Rozanne L. Ridgway, Assistant Secretary of Defense Richard N. Perle, National Security Council officials Jack F. Matlock, Jr. and Robert E. Linhard, and Deputy Assistant Secretary of State Mark Palmer. On the Soviet team were the head of the Foreign Ministry's American Department, Alexander Bessmertnykh; the chief Soviet arms negotiator, Ambassador Viktor Karpov; and Oleg M. Sokolov, Minister-Counselor in the Soviet Embassy in Washington. The crucial issues were discussed by Shultz and Eduard Sheverdnadze, the new Soviet foreign minister, in a series of four meetings ending with Shultz's trip to Moscow in early November.

But the gulf between the two superpowers on the crucial question of arms control had been so wide that without a conceptual breakthrough it was not possible to set a meaningful agenda or to discuss the preconditions of both sides.[1] Hence, the failure at Geneva was guaranteed by the absence of an agreed conceptual framework; both sides ultimately decided to treat the summit as a get-acquainted session that would be the first step in a new process. This, plus the fact that when the time came Reagan and Gorbachev tossed aside the agenda and positions carefully structured by their professional aides, made the Geneva summit extraordinary in terms of the mechanics.

---

[1] Don Oberdorfer quoted a Shultz aide as saying that the two sides could not reach accord on a final communiqué—"They had a communiqué and we had a communiqué, and it was clear there was nothing in between." *Washington Post*, November 6, 1985, p. 1.

So what did the summit accomplish? What is likely to happen at the next summit?

Both sides professed to be satisfied about restarting dialogue, although it seemed clear that this would be a different type of dialogue. Reagan's refusal to abandon the Strategic Defense Initiative meant that the world of "stable nuclear deterrence"—a world essentially without defenses against missile attacks—was being called into question. Moreover, the reluctance to curtail SDI meant the virtual impossibility of achieving an agreement on deep cuts in offensive strategic weapons.

Ironically, it was the United States that had sought to persuade the Russians at the onset of arms control talks in 1967 to abandon their own strategic defense systems based on anti-ballistic missile defenses. As Gordon Weihmiller recounts in chapter 3, President Johnson and his defense secretary, Robert S. McNamara, tried to convince a skeptical Soviet Premier Alexei Kosygin at the 1967 Glassboro summit that anti-ballistic missile defenses would only accelerate the arms race—the same argument Gorbachev was making to Reagan.[2]

It had taken five years to persuade the Russians to abandon their strategic defenses and accept the principle of stable nuclear deterrence based on mutually assured destruction. At Geneva, the two superpowers went back to square one, this time reversing their roles on the concept of deterrence.

The 1985 Geneva summit, in fact, resembled the 1955 Geneva summit more than subsequent high-level meetings in terms of the primary elements of the process outlined in this book. It was a meeting without a specific agenda, a meeting without bargaining.

The only traditional diplomatic negotiating that took

---

[2]Adam Yarmolinski, "Unhappy Irony," *Baltimore Sun*, November 27, 1985, p. 27.

place involved the contents of the joint 'statement' that was issued in the name of the two leaders at the closing ceremonies of the summit. (The designation 'communiqué' was deliberately not used.) Up to the previous evening, differences were such that both sides threatened not to go through with the closing ceremonies. According to an American participant, the impasse was broken by Gorbachev and Shultz. Following the last formal bilateral session, according to this account, Reagan had already left the building when Gorbachev and Shultz encountered one another in the large stairwell, went to an empty room and decided the shape of the joint document in a matter of minutes. Subsequently, American and Soviet members of the working group spent the night hammering out the wording of the document. When they completed the job, it was past four o'clock in the morning, only hours before Reagan and Gorbachev were scheduled to face the television cameras together at the closing ceremony.

The agreed document, in essence, restated the Soviet-American joint statement of the preceding January. It restated Reagan's interest in deep cuts in strategic weapons and an agreement on medium-range nuclear arms in Europe, but made no mention of defensive weapons as envisaged by the SDI. The United States accepted Moscow's wording that the two sides had agreed not to seek "military superiority." The Russian insistence on an assertion about the "inadmissibility of nuclear war" was replaced by acceptance of Reagan's often-used phrase—that a nuclear war "cannot be won and must not be fought."

It was not clear whether the two leaders, who spent a lot of time talking privately to each other, had even attempted to explore ways of regulating their rivalry on a new basis that could accommodate profound divisions on the crucial aspect of their relations. From their public statements it was clear that Reagan advocated his new concept of deterrence, but it was not clear whether Gorbachev would be prepared eventually to go along. He said he was against the idea; that is Moscow's position, at least for the time being. But even under the best of circumstances, it would take specialists from both sides to translate fireside chats into a conceptual framework acceptable to the two countries.

Yet the process started at Geneva could conceivably create a momentum of its own.

It was already apparent at this writing that the shrill rhetoric of the past years had faded away. On January 1, 1986, Reagan and Gorbachev exchanged simultaneously televised New Year's messages and talked to each other's people with a degree of optimism about safeguarding peace. With a relative air of civility restored, it was conceivable that the pressure of the deadline could force both bureaucracies to seek common ground on the fundamental question of strategic relations before Gorbachev's arrival in Washington later in 1986. The two leaders had, in effect, settled most of the mechanical aspects of the next summit; which meant that the two bureaucracies would have to concentrate on the agenda, or the substantive part of negotiations.

Both sides were facing their own budgetary crunches. The Russians did not hide their preoccupation with overcoming the stagnation of their economy and their aversion to seeing huge amounts of rubles sunk into Soviet countermeasures to Reagan's SDI. While Reagan wanted to increase military outlays, pressures in Congress to balance the budget may yet lead to more cuts in the defense program.

But without high-level instructions, the bureaucrats are not likely to accomplish very much. And high-level instructions mandate high-level decisions on the fundamental issues of arms control, or more specifically, the essential framework for negotiations without which all other efforts to deal with strategic and space weapons would be meaningless. As Leslie Gelb put it, it was easy for the two leaders to walk away from their first summit with only handshakes and pledges to strengthen the diplomatic process; after five years of acrimony, the fact that the two superpowers were again on speaking terms was a source of satisfaction in both East and West.[3]

Next time, however, Reagan and Gorbachev would have to make some real movement on the arms control front or risk failure. Domestic political considerations both in Washington and in Moscow were likely to shape the outcome of the next summit more than anything else. What the bureaucracies could do in the absence of an agreed conceptual framework on strategic and space weapons would be to make some headway on such issues as controlling chemical weapons or pushing for accommodation at the MBFR talks in Vienna and the Stockholm East-West disarmament conference. That, at least, would keep the process moving forward while the two sides struggled to find a general framework for the future.

---

[3]*New York Times*, November 27, 1985, p. 14.

Appendix

Chronology, Synopses and Final Documents
of U.S.-Soviet Summit Meetings
1955 to 1985

Chronology

1. **18–23 July 1955:** The Geneva Conference of Heads of Government (Eisenhower, Bulganin, Khrushchev, Eden, and Faure)

2. **15–27 September 1959:** State Visit of Khrushchev and Camp David Discussions (Eisenhower and Khrushchev)

3. **16–17 May 1960:** The Paris Heads of Government Conference (Eisenhower, Khrushchev, de Gaulle, and Macmillan)

4. **3–4 June 1961:** The Vienna Summit (Kennedy and Khrushchev)

5. **23–25 June 1967:** The Glassboro Discussions (Johnson and Kosygin)

6. **22–30 May 1972:** The Moscow Summit and State Visit (Nixon and Brezhnev)

7. **18–25 June 1973:** The Washington/San Clemente Discussions and State Visit (Nixon and Brezhnev)

8. **27 June–3 July 1974:** The Moscow Summit and State Visit (Nixon and Brezhnev)

9. **23–24 November 1974:** The Vladivostok Meetings (Ford and Brezhnev)

10. **15–18 June 1979:** The Vienna Summit (Carter and Brezhnev)

11. **19–21 November 1985:** The Geneva Summit (Reagan and Gorbachev)

Synopses and Final Documents

1. The Geneva Conference of Heads of Government: 18–23 July 1955

Location   Palais des Nations (former Headquarters of the League of Nations).

Initiation   Prime Minister Churchill, May 11, 1953, speaking in the House of Commons, called for "another talk with Soviet Russia upon the highest level" and declared that it was a mistake to "assume that nothing can be settled with Soviet Russia unless or until everything is settled."

Rationale   1955: an easing of tensions in East-West relations.

Principals
U.S.:   President Eisenhower (Conference Chairman), Secretary of State Dulles
U.K.:   Prime Minister Eden, Foreign Secretary Macmillan
France: Premier Faure, Foreign Minister Pinay
USSR: Premier Bulganin (nominal Head of Delegation), CPSU First Secretary Khrushchev, Foreign Minister Molotov, Deputy Foreign Minister Gromyko, Defense Minister Marshal Zhukov

Background   Nuclear stalemate; growing awareness and dangers of massive retaliation. German independence (May 5, 1955) and entry into NATO. Warsaw Pact formed May 15, 1955 in response to above. Soviets suddenly conclude Austrian State Treaty on May 15, 1955. Eisenhower's preconditions and Dulles' skepticism.

Preparation Western foreign ministers hold discussions with Molotov in Vienna on May 15, 1955, followed by mid-June meetings in New York and follow-up meeting with Molotov in San Francisco later in the month. Agreement on procedures (location and duration) but differences on agenda—Dulles: disarmament, German unification, Eastern Europe, aims of international communism; Molotov: disarmament, European security and economic cooperation.

Agreed-upon objective: to define crucial world problems. Exchange of Notes completed June 13, 1955.

Extensive U.S. preparations: position papers and logistics. Extensive coordination among Western allies.

Discussions Marked by "formality and tedium." Agenda not agreed upon until day of opening session. Informal contacts found useful.

Issues Disarmament: Eisenhower's exchange of blueprints and "Open Skies." Germany: unification was nonnegotiable issue. Security: Bulganin's 26-state European security treaty, pledges of non-aggression and eventual dissolution of NATO and Warsaw Pact. East-West contacts: West—free movement of people; Soviets—trade and communication.

Results No formal agreements. Final communiqué in form of a directive to the foreign ministers to undertake negotiations on above issues in Geneva starting in October. These talks subsequently collapsed. Speculation about "the Spirit of Geneva." Eisenhower's evaluation: "limited success."

Directive to Foreign Ministers, Geneva, July 23, 1955[1]

The Heads of Government of France, the United Kingdom, the U.S.S.R. and the U.S.A., guided by the desire to contribute to the relaxation of international tension and to the consolidation of confidence between states, instruct their Foreign Ministers to continue the consideration of the following questions with regard to which an exchange of views has taken place at the Geneva Conference, and to propose effective means for their solution, taking account of the close link between the reunification of Germany and the problems of European security, and the fact that the successful settlement of each of these problems would serve the interests of consolidating peace.

1. *European Security and Germany.* For the purpose of establishing European security with due regard to the legitimate interests of all nations and their inherent right to individual and collective self-defence, the Ministers are instructed to consider various proposals to this end, including the following: A security pact for Europe or for a part of Europe, including provision for the assumption by member nations of an obligation not to resort to force and to deny assistance to an aggressor; limitation, control, and inspection in regard to armed forces and armaments; establishment between East and West of a zone in which the disposition of armed forces will be subject to mutual agreement; and also to consider other possible proposals pertaining to the solution of this problem.

The Heads of Government, recognizing their common responsibility for the settlement of the German question and the re-unification of Germany, have agreed the settlement of the German question and the re-unification of Germany by means of free elections shall be carried out in conformity with the national interests of the German people and the interests of European security. The Foreign Ministers will make whatever arrangements they may consider desirable for the participation of, or for consultation with, other interested parties.

2. *Disarmament*
The Four Heads of Government,

---

[1]*Department of State Bulletin*, Vol. 33, No. 840 (August 1, 1955), pp. 176–77.

Desirous of removing the threat of war and lessening the burden of armaments,

Convinced of the necessity, for secure peace and for the welfare of mankind, of achieving a system for the control and reduction of all armaments and armed forces under effective safeguards,

Recognizing that achievements in this field would release vast material resources to be devoted to the peaceful economic development of nations, for raising their well-being, as well as for assistance to underdeveloped countries,

Agree:

(1) for these purposes to work together to develop an acceptable system for disarmament through the Sub-Committee of the United Nations Disarmament Commission;

(2) to instruct their representatives in the Sub-Committee in the discharge of their mandate from the United Nations to take account in their work of the views and proposals advanced by the Heads of Government at this Conference;

(3) to propose that the next meeting of the Sub-Committee be held on August 29, 1955, at New York;

(4) to instruct the Foreign Ministers to take note of the proceedings in the Disarmament Commission, to take account of the views and proposals advanced by the Heads of Government at this Conference and to consider whether the four Governments can take any further useful initiative in the field of disarmament.

3. *Development of Contacts between East and West*

The Foreign Ministers should by means of experts study measures, including those possible in organs and agencies of the United Nations, which could (a) bring about a progressive elimination of barriers which interfere with free communications and peaceful trade between people and (b) bring about such freer contacts and exchanges as are to the mutual advantage of the countries and peoples concerned.

4. The Foreign Ministers of the Four Powers will meet at Geneva during October to initiate their consideration of these questions and to determine the organisation of their work.

2. State Visit of Khrushchev and Camp David Discussions: 15–27 September 1959

Itinerary   Washington (15–16), New York (17–18), Los Angeles (19), San Francisco (20–21), Des Moines and Ames (22–23), Pittsburgh (24), Camp David (25–27). Accompanied by Ambassador Henry Cabot Lodge.

Initiation   Invitation from President Eisenhower for talks as "a prelude to a summit."

Rationale   Aftermath of second Berlin crisis, deadlock in Geneva foreign ministers' talks, no summit under Soviet threats.

Principals   Camp David discussions—

   U.S.:   President Eisenhower, Vice President Nixon, Secretary of State Herter, Ambassador Lodge, Foy Kohler, (Deputy Assistant Secretary of State for European Affairs).

   USSR: Premier Khrushchev, Foreign Minister Gromyko, Ambassador Menshikov, Soldatov (Chief, American Department, Ministry of Foreign Affairs).

Background   Khrushchev's six-month ultimatum of November 27, 1958 on Berlin and threat to sign a separate peace treaty with East Germany; Khrushchev's strong desire for a summit. Deadlock at Geneva Foreign Ministers' Conferences (May 11–June 20 and July 13–August 5, 1959). Soviets stop nuclear development assistance to China in June 1959.

Preparation   Extensive correspondence between President Eisenhower and Soviet leaders dating back to Premier Bulganin's proposal of December 10, 1957 for an East-West Summit. Eisenhower generally insisted on three preconditions: 1) adequate preparation by foreign ministers, 2) an acceptable agenda agreement in advance, and 3) a reasonable assurance that a summit would result in successful agreements. Extensive coordination with Western allies.

Issues   Discussions focused on German problem resulting in agreement to resume talks on Berlin without time constraints imposed by Soviets. Disarmament (control and inspection), trade and credits, nuclear test ban.

Results   Joint communiqué affirming constructive efforts toward general disarmament, peaceful resolution of international problems, renewal of Berlin negotiations, and invitation for the president to visit the Soviet Union. Eisenhower's consent to an East-West summit conference.

Joint Communiqué, Camp David, September 27, 1959[2]

The Chairman of the Council of Ministers of the U.S.S.R., N.S. Khrushchev, and President Eisenhower have had a frank exchange of opinions at Camp David. In some of these conversations United States Secretary of State Herter and Soviet Foreign Minister Gromyko, as well as other officials from both countries, participated.

Chairman Khrushchev and the President have agreed that these discussions have been useful in clarifying each other's position on a number of subjects. The talks were not undertaken to negotiate issues. It is hoped, however, that their exchanges of views will contribute to a better understanding of the motives and position of each and thus to the achievement of a just and lasting peace.

The Chairman of the Council of Ministers of the U.S.S.R. and the President of the United States agreed that the question of general disarmament is the most important one facing the world today. Both governments will make every effort to achieve a constructive solution of this problem.

In the course of the conversations an exchange of views took place on the question of Germany including the question of a peace treaty with Germany, in which the positions of both sides were expounded.

With respect to the specific Berlin question, an understanding was reached, subject to the approval of the other parties directly concerned, that negotiations would be reopened with a view to achieving a solution which would be in accordance with the interests of all concerned and in the interest of the maintenance of peace.

---

[2]White House (Gettysburg, Pa.), press release dated September 27, in *Department of State Bulletin*, Vol. 41, No. 1049 (October 12, 1959), pp. 499–500.

In addition to these matters useful conversations were held on a number of questions affecting the relations between the Union of Soviet Socialist Republics and the United States. These subjects included the question of trade between the two countries. With respect to an increase in exchanges of persons and ideas, substantial progress was made in discussions between officials and it is expected that certain agreements will be reached in the near future.

The Chairman of the Council of Ministers of the U.S.S.R. and the President of the United States agreed that all outstanding international questions should be settled not by the application of force but by peaceful means through negotiation.

Finally it was agreed that an exact date for the return visit of the President to the Soviet Union next spring would be arranged through diplomatic channels.

3. The Paris Heads of Government Conference: 16–17 May 1960

Location Elyseé Palace.

Initiation Long-standing Soviet desire for an East-West summit consented to by President Eisenhower at Camp David talks. Western letters of 21 December 1959 proposing summit meeting in Paris.

Rationale German problem, arms limitations and nuclear test ban.

Principals
  U.S.: President Eisenhower
  U.K.: Prime Minister Macmillan
  France: President de Gaulle (Host)
  USSR: Premier Khrushchev, Foreign Minister Gromyko, Marshal Malinovsky

Background Following Camp David, improved relations: U.S.-Soviet cultural exchange agreement of November 21, 1959 and Antarctic Treaty of December 1, 1959. Khrushchev's renewed threats to sign a separate German peace treaty in speech to the Supreme Soviet on January 14, 1960; Warsaw Pact commitment on February 4 to sign separate G.D.R. peace treaty; Khrushchev's threats in Baku speech on April 25, and during Paris visit (March 23–April 2). Downing of U-2 on May 1 near Sverdlovsk and ensuing events.

Preparation Western heads of state and government meeting at Rambouillet on 19–21 December 1959. Ministerial meeting of North Atlantic Council reaffirmed position on Berlin the next day.

Discussions Collapse of conference over U-2 incident. Khrushchev arrived in Paris on May 14 and presented de Gaulle with a memo of conditions Eisenhower would have to meet before Khrushchev would attend the summit.

Demands Khrushchev demanded that Eisenhower: 1) publicly apologize for the U-2 espionage flights, 2) condemn those responsible, and 3) announce the end of such flights as aggression against the Soviet Union.

Response   Eisenhower stated that the flights were not aggressive in nature but rather necessary to protect the U.S. and the West from surprise attack; he had previously announced a suspension in further flights.

Results   Collapse of conference and withdrawal of Soviet invitation for Eisenhower to visit the Soviet Union. This was the last attempt at a combined Western allied approach to Soviets at summit conferences.

Western Communiqué, Paris, May 17, 1960[3]

The President of the United States, the President of the French Republic and the Prime Minister of the United Kingdom take note of the fact that because of the attitude adopted by the Chairman of the Council of Ministers of the Soviet Union it has not been possible to begin, at the Summit Conference, the examination of the problems which it had been agreed would be discussed between the four Chiefs of State or Government.

They regret that these discussions, so important for world peace, could not take place. For their part, they remain unshaken in their conviction that all outstanding international questions should be settled not by the use or threat of force but by peaceful means through negotiation. They themselves remain ready to take part in such negotiations at any suitable time in the future.

[3]White House (Paris), press release dated May 17, in *Department of State Bulletin*, Vol. 42, No. 1093 (June 6, 1960), pp. 905–6.

President's Remarks, Washington, May 20, 1960[4]

My good friends and fellow citizens: After a trip of this kind you can well understand what it means to me to have this kind of a welcome. I am deeply appreciative of the trouble that each of you took to come out to this spot. It truly means a lot to me.

As we planned for the summit the hopes of the world were not too high. The experience of the past years had denied us any right to believe that great advances toward the purpose we seek—peace with justice—could be achieved in any great measure. Yet it seems that the identity of interest between ourselves and the Soviets in certain features was so obvious that logically we should have made some progress.

Certainly the subjects on which we wanted to talk were those that seemed so important to them, for example, disarmament, the widening of contacts so that we would have open societies—or slightly more open societies—dealing with each other, then the matter of Berlin and a divided Germany, and finally, as between Russia, the U.K., and ourselves, some agreement on a plan for control of nuclear testing.

Therefore it was a mystery—and remains a mystery—as to why at this particular moment the Soviets chose so to distort and overplay the U-2 incident that they obviously wanted no talks of any kind and, in fact, made it impossible to begin them. I am not going to speculate today as to the future, but it is quite clear that, since they wanted no talks whatsoever at this time, we can be watchful for more irritations, possibly other incidents that can be more than annoying, sometimes creating real problems.

For example, just today a half hour before I landed, it was reported to me that there is a C-47 missing in Western Germany. This is an unarmed, slow plane—no possibility of being used for military purposes—and in fact, I believe it had nine passengers aboard. There was some bad weather, and its route took it near the Eastern German border. We do not know at this moment that any deliberate act delayed it, but at least it is overdue. And so, in the atmosphere in which we now have to think and live, we cannot be sure that the worst has not happened.

---

[4]White House press release dated May 20, in *Department of State Bulletin*, Vol. 42, No. 1093 (June 6, 1960), pp. 906–7. Remarks made at Andrews Air Force Base, Maryland.

Now, I may want to talk soon to the Nation about these matters, and for that part of it, I now stop. But I do want to tell all of you people about three or four encouraging features that I encountered. First of all was the assurance of the support of the home folks: from friends, and from the Joint Chiefs of Staff, from the political leaders of both parties, from newspapers comments and editorial comment of every kind, I was assured of the essential solidarity of the United States and the sincerity of our peaceful purposes.

Secondly was the conduct of my two principal colleagues of the West. Mr. Macmillan and General de Gaulle were superb. They spoke with one voice with our delegation in support of those things which we thought right and decent and logical.

Thirdly was an action on the part of the NATO Council yesterday when Secretary Herter reported to them while I was in Portugal. The NATO resolution unanimously supported the three Western Powers in what we were trying to do.

And finally, the Portuguese reception—in a way I think they wanted to provide the United States and the West, and even me personally, with something of an antidote for some of the disappointments we have felt. Government and citizens alike tried to outdo themselves in the warmth and cordiality of their reception, and, on top of that, in their assurances from every side—newspapers, the officials, common people coming in who were serving us in the Palace—everywhere they said the West in effect is right and we want you to know it. And they used every possible way to do it. And for that day in Portugal yesterday I am grateful.

Finally, since most of you will understand that by our time here it was 1 o'clock when I arose this morning, I am sure you expected nothing of eloquence. But I did want sincerely to give you some of my reactions, convictions as of this moment, and to say again to each of you: Thank you very much indeed.

4. The Vienna Summit: 3–4 June 1961

Initiation   Arranged through diplomatic channels in March.

Rationale   Mutual assessment and frank discussion of divisive issues.

Principals
  U.S.:   President Kennedy
  USSR: Premier Khrushchev

Background Deadlock in Geneva conference on nuclear test ban. Khrushchev's speech of Jan. 6, 1961 on "wars of national liberation." Bay of Pigs fiasco (April 17, 1961). Soviet "troika" proposal to replace U.N. Secretary General.

Preparation President Kennedy's state visit to Paris (May 31–June 2). Subsequent discussions in London with Prime Minister Macmillan (June 4–5).

Discussions Frank, somber . . . brutal.

President Kennedy: 1) Establish a rational basis for accommodation, 2) introduce precision into each other's assessments, 3) avoid miscalculations leading to confrontations.

Premier Khrushchev: Peaceful coexistence and wars of national liberation.

Issues   Nuclear test ban, disarmament, Germany, Laos.

Results   No formal agreement. Communiqué of June 4 affirmed mutual support for a neutral and independent Laos and effective cease-fire.

No progress made toward agreement on nuclear testing/ inspection issue.

Germany and Berlin: no change in previous positions; renewal of Soviet threats of signing separate peace treaty with the G.D.R. within six months. Berlin Wall started August 13, 1961.

Khrushchev: the classical mode of totalitarian diplomacy
by threat and intimidation?

Soviet resumption of atmospheric nuclear testing in
August.

U.S.-USSR Communiqué, Vienna, June 4, 1961[5]

President Kennedy and Premier Khrushchev have concluded two days
of useful meetings, during which they have reviewed the relationships
between the U.S. and the U.S.S.R., as well as other questions that are of
interest to the two States. Today, in the company of their advisors, they
discussed the problems of nuclear testing, disarmament, and Germany.
The President and the Chairman reaffirmed their support of a neutral
and independent Laos under a government chosen by the Laotians
themselves, and of international agreements for insuring that neutrality
and independence, and in this connection they have recognized the
importance of an effective cease-fire. The President and the Chairman
have agreed to maintain contact on all questions of interest to the two
countries and for the whole world.

---

[5]White House (Vienna), press release dated June 4, in *Department of State Bulletin*, Vol.
44, No. 1148 (June 26, 1961), p. 999.

5. The Glassboro Discussions: 23–25 June 1967

Location   "Hollybush," Glassboro State College, New Jersey.

Rationale   General context included Middle East War, Vietnam War and nuclear nonproliferation.

Principals

  U.S.:   President Johnson, Secretary of State Rusk, Secretary of Defense McNamara, Ambassador Thompson.

  USSR: Premier Kosygin, Foreign Minister Gromyko, Ambassador Dobrynin.

Background   President Johnson's "bridge-building" speech of October 1966. Outer Space Treaty signed Jan. 27, 1967; ongoing negotiations on nuclear nonproliferation and Geneva Eighteen-Nation Disarmament Commission. Middle East Crisis of May and "Six-Day War" in June 1967.

Initiation   Meeting to take place during Premier Kosygin's attendance at Fifth Emergency Special Session of the U.N. General Assembly.

Preparation Short lead time. Premier Kosygin reluctant to meet in Washington, dispute over location. Administrative and logistical arrangements made in hectic last 12-hour rush before the meeting.

Discussions Useful, although differences were not resolved. U.S. concern about Soviet ABM system around Moscow.

Issues   Middle East (Six-Day War): Soviet insistence on prompt Israeli withdrawal. Vietnam War: Soviet insistence on an end to bombing of North, U.S. withdrawal. Nonproliferation: general agreement on the importance of this issue.

Results   No formal agreement signed on above issues, no communiqué. Statements.

                 Secretary of Defense McNamara's discussion of strategic negotiations and stabilizing deterrence. Raised U.S. concern about relationship between defensive and offensive strategic missiles and impact on stability.

President's Report to the Nation, Washington, June 25, 1967[6]

On my return tonight to the White House after 2 days of talks at Hollybush, I want to make this brief report to the American people.

We continued our discussions today in the same spirit in which we began them on Friday—a spirit of direct face-to-face exchanges between leaders with very heavy responsibilities.

We wanted to meet again because the issues before us are so large and so difficult that one meeting together was not nearly enough. The two meetings have been better than one, and at least we learned—I know I did—from each hour of our talks.

You will not be surprised to know that these two meetings have not solved all of our problems. On some, we have made progress—great progress in reducing misunderstanding, I think, and in reaffirming our common commitment to seek agreement.

I think we made that kind of progress, for example, on the question of arms limitation. We have agreed this afternoon that Secretary of State Rusk and Mr. Gromyko will pursue this subject further in New York in the days ahead.

I must report that no agreement is readily in sight on the Middle Eastern crisis and that our well-known differences over Viet-Nam continue. Yet even on these issues, I was very glad to hear the Chairman's views face to face and to have a chance to tell him directly and in detail just what our purposes and our policies are—and are not— in these particular areas.

The Chairman, I believe, made a similar effort with me.

When nations have deeply different positions, as we do on these issues, they do not come to agreement merely by improving their understanding of each other's views. But such improvement helps. Sometimes in such discussions you can find elements—beginnings— hopeful fractions—of common ground, even within a general dis- agreement.

It was so in the Middle East 2 weeks ago when we agreed on the need for a prompt cease-fire. And it is so today in respect to such simple

---

[6]White House press release dated June 25, in *Department of State Bulletin* Vol. 57, No. 1463 (July 10, 1967), pp. 37–38.

propositions as that every state has a right to live, that there should be an end to the war in the Middle East, and that in the right circumstances there should be withdrawal of troops. This is a long way from agreement, but it is a long way also from total difference.

On Viet-Nam, the area of agreement is smaller. It is defined by the fact that the dangers and the difficulties of any one area must never be allowed to become a cause of wider conflict. Yet even in Viet-Nam, I was able to make it very clear, with no third party between us, that we will match and we will outmatch every step to peace that others may be ready to take.

As I warned on Friday [June 23]—and as I just must warn again on this Sunday afternoon [June 25]—meetings like these do not themselves make peace in the world. We must all remember that there have been many meetings before and they have not ended all of our troubles or all of our dangers.

But I can also report on this Sunday afternoon another thing that I said on last Friday: That it does help a lot to sit down and look at a man right in the eye and try to reason with him, particularly if he is trying to reason with you.

We may have differences and difficulties ahead, but I think they will be lessened, and not increased, by our new knowledge of each other.

Chairman Kosygin and I have agreed that the leaders of our two countries will keep in touch in the future, through our able secretaries and ambassadors, and also keep in touch directly.

I said on Friday that the world is very small and very dangerous. Tonight I believe that it is fair to say that these days at Hollybush have made it a little smaller still—but also a little less dangerous.

Statement by Premier Kosygin at His News Conference at UN Headquarters, June 25, 1967[7]

On June 25 a second meeting between the Chairman of the Council of Ministers of the U.S.S.R., Mr. Kosygin, and President Johnson of the United States, was held in the town of Glassboro, not far from New

---

[7]*Department of State Bulletin*, Vol. 57, No. 1463 (July 10, 1967), p. 38. Unofficial Translation.

York. At the second meeting, as at the first, which took place on June 23, the exchange of views touched upon several international problems.

In connection with the situation in the Middle East, the two sides set forth their respective positions. It was stated on the Soviet side that the main thing now is to achieve the prompt withdrawal behind the armistice lines of the forces of Israel, which has committed aggression against the Arab states. This question is of signal importance for the restoration of peace in the Middle East, and it is in the center of the attention of the emergency special session of the General Assembly of the United Nations, and it must be positively resolved without delay.

The exchange of views on the Viet-Nam problem once again revealed profound differences in the positions of the Soviet Union and the United States. It was emphasized on the Soviet side that settlement of the Viet-Nam problem is possible only on the condition of an end to the bombing of the territory of the Democratic Republic of Viet-Nam and the withdrawal of American forces from South Viet-Nam.

Both sides reaffirmed that they believe it important to promptly achieve understanding on the conclusion of an international treaty on the nonproliferation of nuclear weapons.

In the course of the talks, a general review was made of the state of bilateral Soviet and American relations. On the whole, the meetings offered the Governments of the Soviet Union and the United States an opportunity to compare their positions on the matters discussed, an opportunity both sides believe to have been useful.

6. The Moscow Summit and State Visit: 22–30 May 1972

Initiation In December 1966 Ambassador Llewellyn Thompson was instructed by President Johnson to propose confidentially to Soviet leaders bilateral talks on strategic arms limitations, notably on antiballistic missile systems.

Rationale To conclude Strategic Arms Limitation Talks (SALT I) Agreement.

Principals

U.S.: President Nixon, Secretary of State Rogers, Assistant to the President for National Security Affairs Kissinger, Ambassador Beam, Assistant Secretary of State for European Affairs Hillenbrand, Assistant to the President Peter Flanigan, Secretary of the Navy Warner; NSC staff: Helmut Sonnenfeldt and William Hyland.

USSR: General Secretary Brezhnev, Chairman of the Presidium of the Supreme Soviet Podgorny, Chairman of the Council of Ministers Kosygin, Foreign Minister Gromyko, Minister of Foreign Trade Patolichev, Deputy Foreign Minister Kuznetsov, Ambassador Dobrynin, Assistant to General Secretary Aleksandrov, others.

Background Favorable Soviet response to U.S. initiative of December 1966 included willingness to negotiate on offensive missile systems, but Soviets delayed start of talks until they achieved parity in ICBMs; Six-Day War of June 1967; Glassboro talks; invasion of Czechoslovakia in August 1968. New initiative by President Nixon led to preliminary SALT talks in Helsinki in November 1969 and more formal negotiations in Vienna and Geneva for next two and a half years (Ambassador Gerard Smith, Director, Arms Control and Disarmament Agency, Deputy Foreign Minister Semenov and Col.-Gen. Ogarkov). Agreed on issues: parity, deterrence and stability. Secret "back channel" negotiations opened by President Nixon in January 1971, involving A/NSA Kissinger with Brezhnev, Kosygin and Amb. Dobrynin. Announcement of SALT breakthrough on May 20, 1971.

Other: Nixon announcement of July 15, 1971, of plan to visit China in February 1972. Soviet-FRG agreement in August 1970 and the Quadripartite Agreement on Germany on September 3, 1971. North Vietnam attack across DMZ on March 30, 1972 and bombing in mid-April of Hanoi and mining of Haiphong harbor.

Preparation   Extensive preliminary discussion (above); U.S./Soviet staffs of about 100; over 500 MEMCONs in 2½ years of discussions; intensive summit preparations. Dr. Kissinger's secret trip to Moscow in April, 1972. Secondary agreements prepared and held for signature at summits.

Discussions   Four levels—plenary and informal sessions, "back channel," and summit meeting. Nixon/Kissinger use of Soviet interpreters; concern for security, bugging. Extensive records of plenary sessions but no transcripts nor verbatim record of summit-level talks, hence, issue of "secret agreements" arose. SALT delegations remained in Helsinki during summit—communication delays.

Results   Treaty on Anti-Ballistic Missile Systems (limit of 2 each); Interim Agreement on Limitation of Strategic Offensive Arms and Protocol thereto; Basic Principles of Relations between the U.S. and U.S.S.R.; Agreements on Environmental Protection, Medical Science and Public Health, Cooperation in Space, Science and Technology, Prevention of Incidents at Sea. First presidential address on Soviet television.

Joint Communiqué, Moscow, May 29, 1972[8]

By mutual agreement between the United States of America and the Union of Soviet Socialist Republics, the President of the United States and Mrs. Richard Nixon paid an official visit to the Soviet Union from

---

[8]White House (Moscow), press release dated May 29, in *Department of State Bulletin*, Vol. 66, No. 1722 (June 26, 1972), pp. 898–902.

May 22 to May 30, 1972. The President was accompanied by Secretary of State William P. Rogers, Assistant to the President Dr. Henry A. Kissinger, and other American officials. During his stay in the USSR President Nixon visited, in addition to Moscow, the cities of Leningrad and Kiev.

President Nixon and L. I. Brezhnev, General Secretary of the Central Committee of the Communist Party of the Soviet Union, N.V. Podgorny, Chairman of the Presidium of the Supreme Soviet of the USSR, and A. N. Kosygin, Chairman of the Council of Ministers of the USSR conducted talks on fundamental problems of American-Soviet relations and the current international situation.

Also taking part in the conversations were:

On the American side: William P. Rogers, Secretary of State; Jacob D. Beam, American Ambassador to the USSR; Dr. Henry A. Kissinger, Assistant to the President for National Security Affairs; Peter M. Flanigan, Assistant to the President; and Martin J. Hillenbrand, Assistant Secretary of State for European Affairs.

On the Soviet side: A. A. Gromyko, Minister of Foreign Affairs of the USSR; N. S. Patolichev, Minister of Foreign Trade; V. V. Kuznetsov, Deputy Minister of Foreign Affairs of the USSR; A. F. Dobrynin, Soviet Ambassador to the USA; A. M. Aleksandrov, Assistant to the General Secretary of the Central Committee, CPSU; G. M. Korniyenko, Member of the Collegium of the Ministry of Foreign Affairs of the USSR.

The discussions covered a wide range of questions of mutual interest and were frank and thorough. They defined more precisely those areas where there are prospects for developing greater cooperation between the two countries, as well as those areas where the positions of the two Sides are different.

I. Bilateral Relations

Guided by the desire to place US-Soviet relations on a more stable and constructive foundation, and mindful of their responsibilities for maintaining world peace and for facilitating the relaxation of international tension, the two Sides adopted a document entitled: "Basic Principles of Mutual Relations between the United States of America and the Union of Soviet Socialist Republics," signed on behalf of the US by President Nixon and on behalf of the USSR by General Secretary Brezhnev.

Both Sides are convinced that the provisions of that document open new possibilities for the development of peaceful relations and mutually beneficial cooperation between the USA and the USSR.

Having considered various areas of bilateral US-Soviet relations, the two Sides agreed that an improvement of relations is possible and desirable. They expressed their firm intention to act in accordance with the provisions set forth in the above-mentioned document.

As a result of progress made in negotiations which preceded the summit meeting, and in the course of the meeting itself, a number of significant agreements were reached. This will intensify bilateral cooperation in areas of common concern as well as in areas relevant to the cause of peace and international cooperation.

Limitation of Strategic Armaments

The two Sides gave primary attention to the problem of reducing the danger of nuclear war. They believe that curbing the competition in strategic arms will make a significant and tangible contribution to this cause.

The two Sides attach great importance to the Treaty on the Limitation of Anti-Ballistic Missile Systems and the Interim Agreement on Certain Measures with Respect to the Limitation of Strategic Offensive Arms concluded between them.[9]

These agreements, which were concluded as a result of the negotiations in Moscow, constitute a major step towards curbing and ultimately ending the arms race.

They are a concrete expression of the intention of the two Sides to contribute to the relaxation of international tension and the strengthening of confidence between states, as well as to carry out the obligations assumed by them in the Treaty on the Non-Proliferation of Nuclear Weapons (Article VI). Both Sides are convinced that the achievement of the above agreements is a practical step towards saving mankind from the threat of the outbreak of nuclear war. Accordingly, it corresponds to the vital interests of the American and Soviet peoples as well as to the vital interests of all other people.

The two Sides intend to continue active negotiations for the limitaton

---

[9]The texts of these two treaties, the "Basic Principles" and the other agreements concluded at the May 1972 summit meeting and touched upon in this joint communiqué are reprinted in full in the *Department of State Bulletin*, Vol. 66, No. 1722 (June 26, 1972), pp. 898–99 and 918–27.

of strategic offensive arms and to conduct them in a spirit of good will, respect for each other's legitimate interests and observance of the principle of equal security.

Both Sides are also convinced that the agreement on Measures to Reduce the Risk of Outbreak of Nuclear War Between the USA and the USSR, signed in Washington on September 30, 1971, serves the interests not only of the Soviet and American peoples, but of all mankind.

Commercial and Economic Relations

Both Sides agreed on measures designed to establish more favorable conditions for developing commercial and other economic ties between the USA and the USSR. The two Sides agree that realistic conditions exist for increasing economic ties. These ties should develop on the basis of mutual benefit and in accordance with generally accepted international practice.

Believing that these aims would be served by conclusion of a trade agreement between the USA and the USSR, the two Sides decided to complete in the near future the work necessary to conclude such an agreement. They agreed on the desirability of credit arrangements to develop mutual trade and of early efforts to resolve other financial and economic issues. It was agreed that a lend-lease settlement will be negotiated concurrently with a trade agreement.

In the interests of broadening and facilitating commercial ties between the two countries, and to work out specific arrangements, the two Sides decided to create a US-Soviet Joint Commercial Commission. Its first meeting will be held in Moscow in the summer of 1972.

Each Side will help promote the establishment of effective working arrangements between organizations and firms of both countries and encouraging [sic] the conclusion of long-term contracts.

Maritime Matters—Incidents at Sea

The two Sides agreed to continue the negotiations aimed at reaching an agreement on maritime and related matters. They believe that such an agreement would mark a positive step in facilitating the expansion of commerce between the United States and the Soviet Union.

An Agreement was concluded between the two Sides on measures to prevent incidents at sea and in air space over it between vessels and aircraft of the US and Soviet Navies. By providing agreed procedures for ships and aircraft of the two navies operating in close proximity, this agreement will diminish the chances of dangerous accidents.

Cooperation in Science and Technology

It was recognized that the cooperation now underway in areas such as atomic energy research, space research, health and other fields benefits both nations and has contributed positively to their over-all relations. It was agreed that increased scientific and technical cooperation on the basis of mutual benefit and shared effort for common goals is in the interest of both nations and would contribute to a further improvement in their bilateral relations. For these purposes the two Sides signed an agreement for cooperation in the fields of science and technology. A US-Soviet Joint Commission on Scientific and Technical Cooperation will be created for identifying and establishing cooperative programs.

Cooperation in Space

Having in mind the role played by the US and the USSR in the peaceful exploration of outer space, both Sides emphasized the importance of further bilateral cooperation in this sphere. In order to increase the safety of man's flights in outer space and the future prospects of joint scientific experiments, the two Sides agreed to make suitable arrangements to permit the docking of American and Soviet spacecraft and stations. The first joint docking experiment of the two countries' piloted spacecraft, with visits by astronauts and cosmonauts to each other's spacecraft, is contemplated for 1975. The planning and implementation of this flight will be carried out by the US National Aeronautics and Space Administration and the USSR Academy of Sciences, according to principles and procedures developed through mutual consultations.

Cooperation in the Field of Health

The two Sides concluded an agreement on health cooperation which marks a fruitful beginning of sharing knowledge about, and collaborative attacks on, the common enemies, disease and disability. The initial research efforts of the program will concentrate on health problems important to the whole world—cancer, heart diseases, and the environmental health sciences. This cooperation subsequently will be broadened to include other health problems of mutual interest. The two Sides pledged their full support for the health cooperation program and agreed to continue the active participation of the two governments in the work of international organizations in the health field.

Environmental Cooperation

The two Sides agreed to initiate a program of cooperation in the protection and enhancement of man's environment. Through joint research and joint measures, the United States and the USSR hope to contribute to the preservation of a healthful environment in their countries and throughout the world. Under the new agreement on environmental cooperation there will be consultations in the near future in Moscow on specific cooperative projects.

Exchanges in the Fields of Science,
Technology, Education, and Culture

Both Sides note the importance of the Agreement on Exchanges and Cooperation in Scientific, Technical, Educational, Cultural, and Other Fields in 1972–1973, signed in Moscow on April 11, 1972. Continuation and expansion of bilateral exchanges in these fields will lead to better understanding and help improve the general state of relations between the two countries. Within the broad framework provided by this Agreement the two Sides have agreed to expand the areas of co-operation, as reflected in new agreements concerning space, health, the environment and science and technology.

The US side, noting the existence of an extensive program of English language instruction in the Soviet Union, indicated its intention to encourage Russian language programs in the United States.

II. INTERNATIONAL ISSUES
Europe

In the course of the discussions on the international situation, both Sides took note of favorable developments in the relaxation of tensions in Europe.

Recognizing the importance to world peace of developments in Europe, where both World Wars originated, and mindful of the responsibilities and commitments which they share with other powers under appropriate agreements, the USA and the USSR intend to make further efforts to ensure a peaceful future for Europe, free of tensions, crises and conflicts.

They agree that the territorial integrity of all states in Europe should be respected.

Both Sides view the September 3, 1971 Quadripartite Agreement relating to the Western Sectors of Berlin as a good example of fruitful cooperation between the states concerned, including the USA and the USSR. The two Sides believe that the implementation of that agreement in the near future, along with other steps, will further improve the European situation and contribute to the necessary trust among states.

Both Sides welcomed the treaty between the USSR and the Federal Republic of Germany signed on August 12, 1970. They noted the significance of the provisions of this treaty as well as of other recent agreements in contributing to confidence and cooperation among the European states.

The USA and the USSR are prepared to make appropriate contributions to the positive trends on the European continent toward a genuine detente and the development of relations of peaceful cooperation among states in Europe on the basis of the principles of territorial integrity and inviolability of frontiers, non-interference in internal affairs, sovereign equality, independence and renunciation of the use or threat of force.

The US and the USSR are in accord that multilateral consultations looking toward a Conference on Security and Cooperation in Europe could begin after the signature of the Final Quadripartite Protocol of the Agreement of September 3, 1971. The two governments agree that the conference should be carefully prepared in order that it may concretely consider specific problems of security and cooperation and thus contribute to the progressive reduction of the underlying causes of tension in Europe. This conference should be convened at a time to be agreed by the countries concerned, but without undue delay.

Both sides believe that the goal of ensuring stability and security in Europe would be served by a reciprocal reduction of armed forces and armaments, first of all in Central Europe. Any agreement on this question should not diminish the security of any of the Sides. Appropriate agreement should be reached as soon as practicable between the states concerned on the procedures for negotiations on this subject in a special forum.

The Middle East

The two Sides set out their positions on this question. They reaffirm their support for a peaceful settlement in the Middle East in accordance with Security Council Resolution 242.

Noting the significance of constructive cooperation of the parties concerned with the Special Representative of the UN Secretary General, Ambassador Jarring, the US and the USSR confirm their desire to contribute to his mission's success and also declare their readiness to play their part in bringing about a peaceful settlement in the Middle East. In the view of the US and the USSR, the achievement of such a settlement would open prospects for the normalization of the Middle East situation and would permit, in particular, consideration of further steps to bring about a military relaxation in that area.

Indochina

Each side set forth its respective standpoint with regard to the continuing war in Vietnam and the situation in the area of Indochina as a whole.

The US side emphasized the need to bring an end to the military conflict as soon as possible and reaffirmed its commitment to the principle that the political future of South Vietnam should be left for the South Vietnamese people to decide for themselves, free from outside interference.

The US side explained its view that the quickest and most effective way to attain the above-mentioned objectives is through negotiations leading to the return of all Americans held captive in the region, the implementation of an internationally supervised Indochina-wide cease-fire and the subsequent withdrawal of all American forces stationed in South Vietnam within four months, leaving the political questions to be resolved by the Indochinese peoples themselves.

The United States reiterated its willingness to enter into serious negotiations with the North Vietnamese Side to settle the war in Indochina on a basis just to all.

The Soviet Side stressed its solidarity with the just struggle of the peoples of Vietnam, Laos and Cambodia for their freedom, independence and social progress. Firmly supporting the proposals of the DRV and the Republic of South Vietnam, which provide a realistic and constructive basis for settling the Vietnam problem, the Soviet Union stands for a cessation of bombings of the DRV, for a complete and unequivocal withdrawal of the troops of the USA and its allies from South Vietnam, so that the peoples of Indochina would have the possibility to determine for themselves their fate without any outside interference.

Disarmament Issues

The two Sides expressed their positions on arms limitation and disarmament issues.

The two Sides note that in recent years their joint and parallel actions have facilitated the working out and conclusion of treaties which curb the arms race or ban some of the most dangerous types of weapons. They note further that these treaties were welcomed by a large majority of the states in the world, which became parties to them.

Both sides regard the Convention on the Prohibition of the Development, Production and Stockpiling of Bacteriological (Biological) and Toxic Weapons and on their Destruction, as an essential disarmament measure. Along with Great Britain, they are the depositories for the Convention which was recently opened for signature by all states. The USA and the USSR will continue their efforts to reach an international agreement regarding chemical weapons.

The USA and the USSR, proceeding from the need to take into account the security interests of both countries on the basis of the principle of equality, and without prejudice to the security interests of third countries, will actively participate in negotiations aimed at working out new measures designed to curb and end the arms race. The ultimate purpose is general and complete disarmament, including nuclear disarmament, under strict international control. A world disarmament conference could play a role in this process at an appropriate time.

Strengthening the United Nations

Both Sides will strive to strengthen the effectiveness of the United Nations on the basis of strict observance of the UN Charter. They regard the United Nations as an instrument for maintaining world peace and security, discouraging conflicts, and developing international cooperation. Accordingly, they will do their best to support United Nations efforts in the interests of international peace.

Both Sides emphasized that agreements and understandings reached in the negotiations in Moscow, as well as the contents and nature of these negotiations, are not in any way directed against any other country. Both Sides proceed from the recognition of the role, the responsibility and the prerogatives of other interested states, existing international obligations and agreements, and the principles and purposes of the UN Charter.

Both Sides believe that positive results were accomplished in the course of the talks at the highest level. These results indicate that despite the differences between the USA and the USSR in social systems, ideologies, and policy principles, it is possible to develop mutually advantageous cooperation between the peoples of both countries, in the interests of strengthening peace and international security.

Both Sides expressed the desire to continue close contact on a number of issues that were under discussion. They agreed that regular consultations on questions of mutual interest, including meetings at the highest level, would be useful.

In expressing his appreciation for the hospitality accorded him in the Soviet Union, President Nixon invited General Secretary L. I. Brezhnev, Chairman N. V. Podgorny, and Chairman A. N. Kosygin to visit the United States at a mutually convenient time. This invitation was accepted.

7. The Washington/San Clemente Discussions and State Visit: 18–25 June 1973

Initiation   President Nixon extended the invitation during his visit to the USSR in May 1972.

Rationale   Détente and continuation of the SALT process.

Principals
  U.S.:   President Nixon, Secretary of State Rogers, Secretary of the Treasury Shultz, A/NSA Kissinger.

  USSR: General Secretary Brezhnev, Foreign Minister Gromyko, Ambassador Dobrynin, Minister of Foreign Trade Patolichev, Minister of Civil Aviation Bugayev, Assistants to the General Secretary Aleksandrov and Tsukanov; Korniyenko, Collegium of the Ministry of Foreign Affairs; Arbatov, USA Institute.

Background   SALT I Agreements of May 1972. Agreement on Ending the War and Restoring Peace in Vietnam, January 27, 1973. Brezhnev's enhanced leadership position; meetings with Pompidou in January 1973 and Brandt in May. Kissinger's Peking trip in February and Sino-American agreement to set up liaison offices in Washington and Peking.

Preparation   Dr. Kissinger's trip to Moscow, May 4–9, 1973. All agreements settled before summit commenced.

Discussions   35 hours of talks; Brezhnev's "shock tactics," useful insights, rapport.

Issues   Reaffirmation of Basic Principles of Relations and strengthening of peaceful ties, prevention of nuclear war, and the SALT process, Germany, Conference on Security and Cooperation in Europe (to convene July 3rd), Middle East, commercial and economic relations, bilateral cooperation.

Results   Joint communiqué of June 24; Brezhnev's television address; invitation to President Nixon to visit the USSR in 1974. The following were signed:

— Agreement on Basic Principles of Negotiation on Strategic Arms Limitation.
— Agreement on Scientific Cooperation in Peaceful Uses of Atomic Energy.
— Agreement on the Prevention of Nuclear War.
— Agreement on Cooperation in Agriculture.
— Agreement on Cooperation in Transportation.
— General Agreement on Contacts, Exchanges and Cooperation.
— Protocols on US-USSR Chamber of Commerce; Commercial Facilities; and Expansion of Air Services.

Joint U.S.-U.S.S.R. Communiqué, San Clemente, June 24, 1973[10]

At the invitation of the President of the United States, Richard Nixon, extended during his official visit to the USSR in May 1972, and in accordance with a subsequent agreement, General Secretary of the Central Committee of the Communist Party of the Soviet Union, Mr. Leonid I. Brezhnev, paid an official visit to the United States from June 18 to June 25. Mr. Brezhnev was accompanied by A. A. Gromyko, Minister of Foreign Affairs of the USSR, Member of the Politbureau of the Central Committee, CPSU; N. S. Patolichev, Minister of Foreign Trade; B. P. Bugayev, Minister of Civil Aviation; G. E. Tsukanov and A. M. Aleksandrov, Assistants to the General Secretary of the Central Committee, CPSU; L. I. Zamyatin, General Director of TASS; E. I. Chazov, Deputy Minister of Public Health of the USSR; G. M. Korniyenko, Member of the Collegium of the Ministry of Foreign Affairs of the USSR; G. A. Arbatov, Director of the USA Institute of the Academy of Sciences of the USSR.

President Nixon and General Secretary Brezhnev held thorough and

---

[10]Signed at San Clemente, Calif., on June 24; released at Moscow, Washington, and San Clemente on June 25. *Department of State Bulletin*, Vol. 69, No. 1778 (July 23, 1973), pp. 130–33.

constructive discussions on the progress achieved in the development of US-Soviet relations and on a number of major international problems of mutual interest.

Also taking part in the conversations held in Washington, Camp David, and San Clemente, were:

On the American side William P. Rogers, Secretary of State; George P. Shultz, Secretary of the Treasury; Dr. Henry A. Kissinger, Assistant to the President for National Security Affairs.

On the Soviet side A. A. Gromyko, Minister of Foreign Affairs of the USSR, Member of Politbureau of the Central Committee, CPSU; A. F. Dobrynin, Soviet Ambassador to the USA; N. S. Patolichev, Minister of Foreign Trade; B. P. Bugayev, Minister of Civil Aviation; A. M. Aleksandrov and G. E. Tsukanov, Assistants to the General Secretary of the Central Committee, CPSU; G. M. Korniyenko, Member of the Collegium of the Ministry of Foreign Affairs of the USSR.

I. The General State of US-Soviet Relations

Both Sides expressed their mutual satisfaction with the fact that the American-Soviet summit meeting in Moscow in May 1972 and the joint decisions taken there have resulted in a substantial advance in the strengthening of peaceful relations between the USA and the USSR and have created the basis for the further development of broad and mutually beneficial cooperation in various fields of mutual interest to the peoples of both countries and in the interests of all mankind. They noted their satisfaction with the mutual effort to implement strictly and fully the treaties and agreements concluded between the USA and the USSR, and to expand areas of cooperation.

They agreed that the process of reshaping relations between the USA and the USSR on the basis of peaceful coexistence and equal security as set forth in the Basic Principles of Relations Between the USA and the USSR signed in Moscow on May 29, 1972 is progressing in an encouraging manner. They emphasized the great importance that each Side attaches to these Basic Principles. They reaffirmed their commitment to the continued scrupulous implementation and to the enhancement of the effectiveness of each of the provisions of that document.

Both Sides noted with satisfaction that the outcome of the US-Soviet meeting in Moscow in May 1972 was welcomed by other States and by world opinion as an important contribution to strengthening peace and international security, to curbing the arms race and to developing businesslike cooperation among States with different social systems.

Both Sides viewed the return visit to the USA of the General Secretary of the Central Committee of the CPSU, L. I. Brezhnev, and the talks held during the visit as an expression of their mutual determination to continue the course toward a major improvement in US-Soviet relations.

Both Sides are convinced that the discussions they have just held represent a further milestone in the constructive development of their relations.

Convinced that such a development of American-Soviet relations serves the interests of both of their peoples and all of mankind, it was decided to take further major steps to give these relations maximum stability and to turn the development of friendship and cooperation between their peoples into a permanent factor for worldwide peace.

II. THE PREVENTION OF NUCLEAR WAR AND THE LIMITATION OF STRATEGIC ARMAMENTS

Issues related to the maintenance and strengthening of international peace were a central point of the talks between President Nixon and General Secretary Brezhnev.

Conscious of the exceptional importance for all mankind of taking effective measures to that end, they discussed ways in which both Sides could work toward removing the danger of war, and especially nuclear war, between the USA and the USSR and between either party and other countries. Consequently, in accordance with the Charter of the United Nations and the Basic Principles of Relations of May 29, 1972, it was decided to conclude an Agreement Between the USA and the USSR on the Prevention of Nuclear War. That Agreement was signed by the President and the General Secretary on June 22, 1973. The text has been published separately.[11]

The President and the General Secretary, in appraising this Agreement, believe that it constitutes a historical landmark in Soviet-American relations and substantially strengthens the foundations of international security as a whole. The United States and the Soviet

---

[11]The text of this and other agreements concluded at the June 1973 summit meeting are reprinted in full in the *Department of State Bulletin*, Vol. 69, No. 1778 (July 23, 1973), pp. 158ff.

Union state their readiness to consider additional ways of strengthening peace and removing forever the danger of war, and particularly nuclear war.

In the course of the meetings, intensive discussions were held on questions of strategic arms limitation. In this connection both Sides emphasized the fundamental importance of the Treaty on the Limitation of Anti-Ballistic Missile Systems and the Interim Agreement on Certain Measures with Respect to the Limitation of Strategic Offensive Arms signed between the USA and the USSR in May 1972 which, for the first time in history, place actual limits on the most modern and most formidable types of armaments.

Having exchanged views on the progress in the implementation of these agreements, both Sides reaffirmed their intention to carry them out and their readiness to move ahead jointly toward an agreement on the future limitation of strategic arms.

Both Sides noted that progress has been made in the negotiations that resumed in November 1972, and that the prospects for reaching a permanent agreement on more complete measures limiting strategic offensive armaments are favorable.

Both Sides agreed that progress made in the limitation of strategic armaments is an exceedingly important contribution to the strengthening of US-Soviet relations and to world peace.

On the basis of their discussions, the President and the General Secretary signed on June 21, 1973, Basic Principles of Negotiations on the Further Limitation of Strategic Offensive Arms. The text has been published separately.

The USA and the USSR attach great importance to joining with all States in the cause of strengthening peace, reducing the burden of armaments, and reaching agreements on arms limitations and disarmament measures.

Considering the important role which an effective international agreement with respect to chemical weapons would play, the two Sides agreed to continue their efforts to conclude such an agreement in cooperation with other countries.

The two Sides agree to make every effort to facilitate the work of the Committee on Disarmament which has been meeting in Geneva. They will actively participate in negotiations aimed at working out new measures to curb and end the arms race. They reaffirm that the ultimate objective is general and complete disarmament, including nuclear disarmament, under strict international control. A world disarmament conference could play a role in this process at an appropriate time.

III. INTERNATIONAL QUESTIONS: THE REDUCTION OF TENSIONS AND STRENGTHENING OF INTERNATIONAL SECURITY

President Nixon and General Secretary Brezhnev reviewed major questions of the current international situation. They gave special attention to the developments which have occurred since the time of the US-Soviet summit meeting in Moscow. It was noted with satisfaction that positive trends are developing in international relations toward the further relaxation of tensions and the strengthening of cooperative relations in the interests of peace. In the opinion of both Sides, the current process of improvement in the international situation creates new and favorable opportunities for reducing tensions, settling outstanding international issues, and creating a permanent structure of peace.

Indochina

The two Sides expressed their deep satisfaction at the conclusion of the Agreement on Ending the War and Restoring Peace in Vietnam, and also at the results of the International Conference on Vietnam which approved and supported that Agreement.

The two Sides are convinced that the conclusion of the Agreement on Ending the War and Restoring Peace in Vietnam, and the subsequent signing of the Agreement on Restoring Peace and Achieving National Concord in Laos, meet the fundamental interests and aspirations of the people of Vietnam and Laos and open up a possibility for establishing a lasting peace in Indochina, based on respect for the independence, sovereignty, unity and territorial integrity of the countries of that area. Both Sides emphasized that these agreements must be strictly implemented.

They further stressed the need to bring an early end to the military conflict in Cambodia in order to bring peace to the entire area of Indochina. They also reaffirmed their stand that the political futures of Vietnam, Laos, and Cambodia should be left to the respective peoples to determine, free from outside interference.

Europe

In the course of the talks both Sides noted with satisfaction that in Europe the process of relaxing tensions and developing cooperation is actively continuing and thereby contributing to international stability.

The two Sides expressed satisfaction with the further normalization of relations among European countries resulting from treaties and agreements signed in recent years, particularly between the USSR and the FRG [Federal Republic of Germany]. They also welcome the coming into force of the Quadripartite Agreement of September 3, 1971. They share the conviction that strict observance of the treaties and agreements that have been concluded will contribute to the security and well-being of all parties concerned.

They also welcome the prospect of United Nations membership this year for the FRG and the GDR [German Democratic Republic] and recall, in this connection, that the USA, USSR, UK and France have signed the Quadripartite Declaration of November 9, 1972, on this subject.

The USA and the USSR reaffirm their desire, guided by the appropriate provisions of the Joint US-USSR Communique adopted in Moscow in May 1972, to continue their separate and joint contributions to strengthening peaceful relations in Europe. Both Sides affirm that ensuring a lasting peace in Europe is a paramount goal of their policies.

In this connection satisfaction was expressed with the fact that as a result of common efforts by many States, including the USA and the USSR, the preparatory work has been successfully completed for the Conference on Security and Cooperation in Europe, which will be convened on July 3, 1973. The USA and the USSR hold the view that the Conference will enhance the possibilities for strengthening European security and developing cooperation among the participating States. The USA and the USSR will conduct their policies so as to realize the goals of the Conference and bring about a new era of good relations in this part of the world.

Reflecting their continued positive attitude toward the Conference, both Sides will make efforts to bring the Conference to a successful conclusion at the earliest possible time. Both Sides proceed from the assumption that progress in the work of the Conference will produce possibilities for completing it at the highest level.

The USA and the USSR believe that the goal of strengthening

stability and security in Europe would be further advanced if the relaxation of political tensions were accompanied by a reduction of military tensions in Central Europe. In this respect they attach great importance to the negotiations on the mutual reduction of forces and armaments and associated measures in Central Europe which will begin on October 30, 1973. Both Sides state their readiness to make, along with other States, their contribution to the achievement of mutually acceptable decisions on the substance of this problem, based on the strict observance of the principle of the undiminished security of any of the parties.

Middle East

The parties expressed their deep concern with the situation in the Middle East and exchanged opinions regarding ways of reaching a Middle East settlement.

Each of the parties set forth its position on this problem.

Both parties agreed to continue to exert their efforts to promote the quickest possible settlement in the Middle East. This settlement should be in accordance with the interests of all states in the area, be consistent with their independence and sovereignty and should take into due account the legitimate interests of the Palestinian people.

IV. Commercial and Economic Relations

The President and the General Secretary thoroughly reviewed the status of and prospects for commercial and economic ties between the USA and the USSR. Both Sides noted with satisfaction the progress achieved in the past year in the normalization and development of commercial and economic relations between them.

They agreed that mutually advantageous cooperation and peaceful relations would be strengthened by the creation of a permanent foundation of economic relationships.

They recall with satisfaction the various agreements on trade and commercial relations signed in the past year. Both Sides note that American-Soviet trade has shown a substantial increase, and that there are favorable prospects for a continued rise in the exchange of goods over the coming years.

They believe that the two countries should aim at a total of 2-3 billion dollars of trade over the next three years. The Joint US-USSR Commercial Commission continues to provide a valuable mechanism to promote the broad-scale growth of economic relations. The two Sides noted with satisfaction that contacts between American firms and their Soviet counterparts are continuing to expand.

Both Sides confirmed their firm intention to proceed from their earlier understanding on measures directed at creating more favorable conditions for expanding commercial and other economic ties between the USA and the USSR.

It was noted that as a result of the Agreement Regarding Certain Maritime Matters signed in October 1972, Soviet and American commercial ships have been calling more frequently at ports of the United States and the USSR, respectively, and since late May of this year a new regular passenger line has started operating between New York and Leningrad.

In the course of the current meeting, the two Sides signed a Protocol augmenting existing civil air relations between the USA and the USSR providing for direct air services between Washington and Moscow and New York and Leningrad, increasing the frequency of flights and resolving other questions in the field of civil aviation.

In the context of reviewing prospects for further and more permanent economic cooperation, both Sides expressed themselves in favor of mutually advantageous long term projects. They discussed a number of specific projects involving the participation of American companies, including the delivery of Siberian natural gas to the United States. The President indicated that the USA encourages American firms to work out concrete proposals on these projects and will give serious and sympathetic consideration to proposals that are in the interest of both Sides.

To contribute to expanded commercial, cultural and technical relations between the USA and the USSR, the two Sides signed a tax convention to avoid double taxation on income and eliminate, as much as possible, the need for citizens of one country to become involved in the tax system of the other.

A Protocol was also signed on the opening by the end of October 1973 of a Trade Representation of the USSR in Washington and a Commercial Office of the United States in Moscow. In addition a Protocol was signed on questions related to establishing a US-Soviet Chamber of Commerce. These agreements will facilitate the further development of commercial and economic ties between the USA and the USSR.

V. Further Progress in Other Fields of Bilateral Cooperation

The two Sides reviewed the areas of bilateral cooperation in such fields as environmental protection, public health and medicine, exploration of outer space, and science and technology, established by the agreements signed in May 1972 and subsequently. They noted that those agreements are being satisfactorily carried out in practice in accordance with the programs as adopted.

In particular, a joint effort is under way to develop effective means to combat those diseases which are most widespread and dangerous for mankind: cancer, cardiovascular or infectious diseases and arthritis. The medical aspects of the environmental problems are also subjects of cooperative research.

Preparations for the joint space flight of the Apollo and Soyuz spacecraft are proceeding according to an agreed timetable. The joint flight of these spaceships for a rendezvous and docking mission, and mutual visits of American and Soviet astronauts in each other's spacecraft, are scheduled for July 1975.

Building on the foundation created in previous agreements, and recognizing the potential of both the USA and the USSR to undertake cooperative measures in current scientific and technological areas, new projects for fruitful joint efforts were identified and appropriate agreements were concluded.

Peaceful Uses of Atomic Energy

Bearing in mind the great importance of satisfying the growing energy demands in both countries and throughout the world, and recognizing that the development of highly efficient energy sources could contribute to the solution of this problem, the President and General Secretary signed an agreement to expand and strengthen cooperation in the fields of controlled nuclear fusion, fast breeder reactors, and research on the fundamental properties of matter. A Joint Committee on Cooperation in the Peaceful Uses of Atomic Energy will be established to implement this agreement, which has a duration of ten years.

Agriculture

Recognizing the importance of agriculture in meeting mankind's requirement for food products and the role of science in modern agricultural production, the two Sides concluded an agreement providing for a broad exchange of scientific experience in agricultural research and development, and of information on agricultural economics. A US-USSR Joint Committee on Agricultural Cooperation will be established to oversee joint programs to be carried out under the Agreement.

World Ocean Studies

Considering the unique capabilities and the major interest of both nations in the field of world ocean studies, and noting the extensive experience of US-USSR oceanographic cooperation, the two Sides have agreed to broaden their cooperation and have signed an agreement to this effect. In so doing, they are convinced that the benefits from further development of cooperation in the field of oceanography will accrue not only bilaterally but also to all peoples of the world. A US-USSR Joint Committee on Cooperation in World Ocean Studies will be established to coordinate the implementation of cooperative programs.

Transportation

The two Sides agreed that there are opportunities for cooperation between the USA and the USSR in the solution of problems in the field of transportation. To permit expanded, mutually beneficial cooperation in this field, the two Sides concluded an agreement on this subject. The USA and the USSR further agreed that a Joint Committee on Cooperation in Transportation would be established.

Contacts, Exchanges and Cooperation

Recognizing the general expansion of US-USSR bilateral relations and, in particular, the growing number of exchanges in the fields of science, technology, education and culture, and in other fields of mutual interest, the two Sides agreed to broaden the scope of these activities under a new General Agreement on Contacts, Exchanges, and Cooperation, with a duration of six years. The two Sides agreed to this in the mutual belief that it will further promote better understanding between the peoples of the United States and the Soviet Union and will help to improve the general state of relations between the two countries.

Both Sides believe that the talks at the highest level, which were held in a frank and constructive spirit, were very valuable and made an important contribution to developing mutually advantageous relations between the USA and the USSR. In the view of both Sides, these talks will have a favorable impact on international relations.

They noted that the success of the discussions in the United States was facilitated by the continuing consultation and contacts as agreed in May 1972. They reaffirmed that the practice of consultation should continue. They agreed that further meetings at the highest level should be held regularly.

Having expressed his appreciation to President Nixon for the hospitality extended during the visit to the United States, General Secretary Brezhnev invited the President to visit the USSR in 1974. The invitation was accepted.

June 24, 1973

RICHARD NIXON

President of the United States of America

LEONID I. BREZHNEV

General Secretary of the Central Committee, CPSU

8. The Moscow Summit and State Visit: 27 June–3 July 1974

Initiation Invitation was extended by General Secretary Brezhnev during his visit to the U.S. in June 1973.

Itinerary Moscow, Minsk, Southern Coast of Crimea.

Principals

U.S.: President and Mrs. Nixon, Secretary of State and A/NSA Kissinger, Ambassador Stoessel; General Haig, Assistant to the President; R. Ziegler, Press Secretary; Major General Scowcroft, Deputy A/NSA; State Department Counselor Sonnenfeldt; Assistant Secretary of State for European Affairs Hartman.

USSR: General Secretary Brezhnev; Chairman of the Presidium of the USSR Supreme Soviet Podgorny; Chairman of the USSR Council of Ministers Kosygin; Foreign Minister Gromyko, Ambassador Dobrynin, Assistant to the General Secretary Aleksandrov, Director General of TASS Zamyatin, Collegium of the Ministry of Foreign Affairs member Korniyenko.

Background Failure to reach agreement during the 1973 summit on ceilings for strategic launchers and MIRVs. Yom Kippur War (October 1973) and strains on détente from Soviet treatment of dissidents. Watergate; perception of discrediting of Nixon's policies.

Preparation Dr. Kissinger's trip to Moscow in March 1974. Stop en route by President Nixon in Brussels for 25th anniversary of NATO and signing of Declaration of Atlantic Relations.

Discussions Thorough and useful; businesslike and constructive atmosphere; more subdued due to impending Watergate results.

Issues Further cooperative efforts, continuation of SALT process, CSCE progress, Middle East, Vietnam, U.N. effectiveness, commercial and economic matters, bilateral cooperative efforts.

Results   Joint communiqué of July 3rd; invitation for Brezhnev to
visit U.S. in 1975; agreed to hold "mini-summit" before
end of 1974 for further negotiations on offensive strategic
missile system limitations. Signature of the following
documents:
— Protocol to the Treaty on the Limitation of Anti-
  Ballistic Systems (reduced from 2 to 1 the number
  permitted).
— Treaty and Protocol on the Limitation of Underground
  Nuclear Weapon Tests.
— Long-Term Agreement on Economic, Industrial, and
  Technical Cooperation.
— Agreements on Cooperation in Energy, Housing,
  Artificial Heart Research.

Joint Communiqué, Moscow, July 3, 1974[12]

In accordance with the agreement to hold regular US-Soviet meetings at
the highest level and at the invitation, extended during the visit of
General Secretary of the Central Committee of the Communist Party of
the Soviet Union L. I. Brezhnev to the USA in June 1973, the President
of the United States of America and Mrs. Richard Nixon paid an
official visit to the Soviet Union from June 27 to July 3, 1974.

During his stay President Nixon visited, in addition to Moscow,
Minsk and the Southern Coast of the Crimea.

The President of the United States and the Soviet leaders held a
thorough and useful exchange of views on major aspects of relations
between the USA and the USSR and on the present international
situation.

On the Soviet side the talks were conducted by L. I. Brezhnev,
General Secretary of the Central Committee of the Communist Party of
the Soviet Union; N. V. Podgorny, Chairman of the Presidium of the
USSR Supreme Soviet; A. N. Kosygin, Chairman of the USSR Council
of Ministers; and A. A. Gromyko, Minister of Foreign Affairs of the
USSR.

---

[12]*Department of State Bulletin*, Vol. 71, No. 1831 (July 29, 1974), pp. 185–91.

Accompanying the President of the USA and participating in the talks was Dr. Henry A. Kissinger, US Secretary of State and Assistant to the President for National Security Affairs.

Also taking part in the talks were:

On the American Side: Walter J. Stoessel, Jr., American Ambassador to the USSR; General Alexander M. Haig, Jr., Assistant to the President; Mr. Ronald L. Ziegler, Assistant to the President and Press Secretary; Major General Brent Scowcroft, Deputy Assistant to the President for National Security Affairs; Mr. Helmut Sonnenfeldt, Counselor of the Department of State; and Mr. Arthur A. Hartman, Assistant Secretary of State for European Affairs.

On the Soviet Side: A. F. Dobrynin, Soviet Ambassador to the USA; A. M. Aleksandrov, Assistant to the General Secretary of the Central Committee, CPSU; L. M. Zamyatin, Director General of TASS; and G. M. Korniyenko, Member of the Collegium of the Ministry of Foreign Affairs of the USSR.

The talks were held in a most businesslike and constructive atmosphere and were marked by a mutual desire of both Sides to continue to strengthen understanding, confidence and peaceful cooperation between them and to contribute to the strengthening of international security and world peace.

I. Progress in Improving US-Soviet Relations

Having considered in detail the development of relations between the USA and the USSR since the US-Soviet summit meeting in May 1972, both Sides noted with satisfaction that through their vigorous joint efforts they have brought about over this short period a fundamental turn toward peaceful relations and broad, mutually beneficial cooperation in the interests of the peoples of both countries and of all mankind.

They emphasized the special importance for the favorable development of relations between the USA and the USSR of meetings of their leaders at the highest level, which are becoming established practice. These meetings provide opportunities for effective and responsible discussion, for the solution of fundamental and important bilateral questions, and for mutual contributions to the settlement of international problems affecting the interests of both countries.

Both Sides welcome the establishment of official contacts between the Congress of the US and the Supreme Soviet of the USSR. They will encourage a further development of such contacts, believing that they can play an important role.

Both Sides confirmed their mutual determination to continue actively to reshape US-Soviet relations on the basis of peaceful coexistence and equal security, in strict conformity with the spirit and the letter of the agreements achieved between the two countries and their obligations under those agreements. In this connection they noted once again the fundamental importance of the joint documents adopted as a result of the summit meetings in 1972 and 1973, especially of the Basic Principles of Relations Between the USA and the USSR, the Agreement on the Prevention of Nuclear War, the Treaty on the Limitation of Anti-Ballistic Missile Systems, and the Interim Agreement on Certain Measures with Respect to the Limitation of Strategic Offensive Arms.

Both Sides are deeply convinced of the imperative necessity of making the process of improving US-Soviet relations irreversible. They believe that, as a result of their efforts, a real possibility has been created to achieve this goal. This will open new vistas for broad mutually beneficial cooperation, and for strengthening friendship between the American and Soviet peoples, and will thus contribute to the solution of many urgent problems facing the world.

Guided by these worthy goals, both Sides decided to continue steadfastly to apply their joint efforts—in cooperation with other countries concerned, as appropriate—first of all in such important fields as:

—removing the danger of war, including particularly war involving nuclear and other mass-destruction weapons;

—limiting and eventually ending the arms race especially in strategic weapons, having in mind as the ultimate objective the achievement of general and complete disarmament under appropriate international control;

—contributing to the elimination of sources of international tension and military conflict;

—strengthening and extending the process of relaxation of tensions throughout the world;

—developing broad, mutually beneficial cooperation in commercial and economic, scientific-technical and cultural fields on the basis of the principles of sovereignty, equality and non-interference in internal affairs with a view to promoting increased understanding and confidence between the peoples of both countries.

Accordingly, in the course of this summit meeting both Sides considered it possible to take new constructive steps which, they believe, will not only advance further the development of US-Soviet relations but will also make a substantial contribution to strengthening world peace and expanding international cooperation.

II. FURTHER LIMITATION OF STRATEGIC ARMS AND OTHER DISARMAMENT ISSUES

Both Sides again carefully analyzed the entire range of their mutual relations connected with the prevention of nuclear war and limitation of strategic armaments. They arrived at the common view that the fundamental agreements concluded between them in this sphere continue to be effective instruments of the general improvement of US-Soviet relations and the international situation as a whole. The USA and the USSR will continue strictly to fulfill the obligations undertaken in those agreements.

In the course of the talks, the two Sides had a thorough review of all aspects of the problem of limitation of strategic arms. They concluded that the Interim Agreement on offensive strategic weapons should be followed by a new agreement between the United States and the Soviet Union on the limitation of strategic arms. They agreed that such an agreement should cover the period until 1985 and deal with both quantitative and qualitative limitations. They agreed that such an agreement should be completed at the earliest possible date, before the expiration of the Interim Agreement.

They hold the common view that such a new agreement would serve not only the interests of the United States and the Soviet Union but also those of a further relaxation of international tensions and of world peace.

Their delegations will reconvene in Geneva in the immediate future on the basis of instructions growing out of the summit.

Taking into consideration the interrelationship between the development of offensive and defensive types of strategic arms and noting the successful implementation of the Treaty on the Limitation of Anti-Ballistic Missile Systems concluded between them in May 1972, both Sides considered it desirable to adopt additional limitations on the deployment of such systems. To that end they concluded a protocol providing for the limitation of each Side to a single deployment area for

ABM Systems instead of two such areas as permitted to each Side by the Treaty.[13]

At the same time, two protocols were signed entitled "Procedures Governing Replacement, Dismantling or Destruction and Notification Thereof, for Strategic Offensive Arms" and "Procedures Governing Replacement, Dismantling or Destruction, and Notification Thereof for ABM Systems and Their Components." These protocols were worked out by the Standing Consultative Commission which was established to promote the objectives and implementation of the provisions of the Treaty and the Interim Agreement signed on May 26, 1972.

The two Sides emphasized the serious importance which the US and USSR also attach to the realization of other possible measures—both on a bilateral and on a multilateral basis—in the field of arms limitation and disarmament.

Having noted the historic significance of the Treaty Banning Nuclear Weapon Tests in the Atmosphere, in Outer Space and Under Water, concluded in Moscow in 1963, to which the United States and the Soviet Union are parties, both Sides expressed themselves in favor of making the cessation of nuclear weapon tests comprehensive. Desiring to contribute to the achievement of this goal the USA and the USSR concluded, as an important step in this direction, the Treaty on the Limitation of Underground Nuclear Weapon Tests providing for the complete cessation, starting from March 31, 1976, of the tests of such weapons above an appropriate yield threshold, and for confining other underground tests to a minimum.

The Parties emphasized the fundamental importance of the Treaty on the Non-Proliferation of Nuclear Weapons. Having reaffirmed their mutual intention to observe the obligations assumed by them under that Treaty, including Article VI thereof, they expressed themselves in favor of increasing its effectiveness.

A joint statement was also signed in which the US and USSR advocate the most effective measures possible to overcome the dangers of the use of environmental modification techniques for military purposes.

---

[13]The text of this treaty and other agreements concluded at the June 1974 summit meeting are reprinted in full in the *Department of State Bulletin*, Vol. 71, No. 1831 (July 29, 1974), pp. 216–23.

Both Sides reaffirmed their interest in an effective international agreement which would exclude from the arsenals of States such dangerous instruments of mass destruction as chemical weapons. Desiring to contribute to early progress in this direction, the USA and the USSR agreed to consider a joint initiative in the Conference of the Committee on Disarmament with respect to the conclusion, as a first step, of an international Convention dealing with the most dangerous, lethal means of chemical warfare.

Both Sides are convinced that the new important steps which they have taken and intend to take in the field of arms limitation as well as further efforts toward disarmament will facilitate the relaxation of international tensions and constitute a tangible contribution to the fulfillment of the historic task of excluding war from the life of human society and thereby of ensuring world peace. The US and the USSR reaffirmed that a world disarmament conference at an appropriate time can play a positive role in this process.

III. PROGRESS IN THE SETTLEMENT OF INTERNATIONAL PROBLEMS

In the course of the meeting detailed discussions were held on major international problems.

Both Sides expressed satisfaction that relaxation of tensions, consolidation of peace, and development of mutually beneficial cooperation are becoming increasingly distinct characteristics of the development of the international situation. They proceed from the assumption that progress in improving the international situation does not occur spontaneously but requires active and purposeful efforts to overcome obstacles and resolve difficulties that remain from the past.

The paramount objectives of all states and peoples should be to ensure, individually and collectively, lasting security in all parts of the world, the early and complete removal of existing international conflicts and sources of tension and the prevention of new ones from arising.

The United States and the Soviet Union are in favor of the broad and fruitful economic cooperation among all states, large and small, on the basis of full equality and mutual benefit.

The United States and the Soviet Union reaffirm their determination to contribute separately and jointly to the achievement of all these tasks.

Europe

Having discussed the development of the situation in Europe since the last American-Soviet summit meeting, both Sides noted with profound satisfaction the further appreciable advances toward establishing dependable relations of peace, goodneighborliness and cooperation on the European continent.

Both sides welcome the major contribution which the Conference on Security and Cooperation in Europe is making to this beneficial process. They consider that substantial progress has already been achieved at the Conference on many significant questions. They believe that this progress indicates that the present stage of the Conference will produce agreed documents of great international significance expressing the determination of the participating states to build their mutual relations on a solid jointly elaborated basis. The US and USSR will make every effort, in cooperation with the other participants, to find solutions acceptable to all for the remaining problems.

Both Sides expressed their conviction that successful completion of the Conference on Security and Cooperation in Europe would be an outstanding event in the interests of establishing a lasting peace. Proceeding from this assumption the USA and the USSR expressed themselves in favor of the final stage of the Conference taking place at an early date. Both Sides also proceed from the assumption that the results of the negotiations will permit the Conference to be concluded at the highest level, which would correspond to the historic significance of the Conference for the future of Europe and lend greater authority to the importance of the Conference's decisions.

Both Sides reaffirmed the lasting significance for a favorable development of the situation in Europe of the treaties and agreements concluded in recent years between European states with different social systems.

They expressed satisfaction with the admission to the United Nations of the Federal Republic of Germany and the German Democratic Republic.

Both Sides also stressed that the Quadripartite Agreement of September 3, 1971, must continue to play a key role in ensuring stability and detente in Europe. The US and USSR consider that the strict and consistent implementation of this Agreement by all parties concerned is an essential condition for the maintenance and strengthening of mutual confidence and stability in the center of Europe.

The USA and the USSR believe that, in order to strengthen stability and security in Europe, the relaxation of political tension on this continent should be accompanied by measures to reduce military tensions.

They therefore attach great importance to the current negotiations on the mutual reduction of forces and armaments and associated measures in Central Europe, in which they are participating. The two Sides expressed the hope that these negotiations will result in concrete decisions ensuring the undiminished security of any of the parties and preventing unilateral military advantages.

Middle East

Both Sides believe that the removal of the danger of war and tension in the Middle East is a task of paramount importance and urgency, and therefore, the only alternative is the achievement, on the basis of UN Security Council Resolution 338, of a just and lasting peace settlement in which should be taken into account the legitimate interests of all peoples in the Middle East, including the Palestinian people, and the right to existence of all states in the area.

As Co-Chairmen of the Geneva Peace Conference on the Middle East, the USA and the USSR consider it important that the Conference resume its work as soon as possible, with the question of other participants from the Middle East area to be discussed at the Conference. Both Sides see the main purpose of the Geneva Peace Conference, the achievement of which they will promote in every way, as the establishment of just and stable peace in the Middle East.

They agreed that the USA and the USSR will continue to remain in close touch with a view to coordinating the efforts of both countries toward a peaceful settlement in the Middle East.

Indochina

Both Sides noted certain further improvements in the situation in Indochina. In the course of the exchange of views on the situation in Vietnam both Sides emphasized that peace and stability in the region can be preserved and strengthened only on the basis of strict observance by all parties concerned of the provisions of the Paris Agreement of January 27, 1973, and the Act of the International Conference on Vietnam of March 2, 1973.

As regards Laos, they noted progress in the normalization of the situation as a result of the formation there of coalition governmental bodies. Both Sides also pronounced themselves in favor of strict fulfillment of the pertinent agreements.

Both Sides also stressed the need for an early and just settlement of the problem of Cambodia based on respect for the sovereign rights of the Cambodian people to a free and independent development without any outside interference.

Strengthening the Role of the United Nations

The United States of America and the Soviet Union attach great importance to the United Nations as an instrument for maintaining peace and security and the expansion of international cooperation. They reiterate their intention to continue their efforts toward increasing the effectiveness of the United Nations in every possible way, including in regard to peacekeeping, on the basis of strict observance of the United Nations Charter.

IV. COMMERCIAL AND ECONOMIC RELATIONS

In the course of the meeting great attention was devoted to a review of the status of and prospects for relations between the USA and the USSR in the commercial and economic field.

Both Sides reaffirmed that they regard the broadening and deepening of mutually advantageous ties in this field on the basis of equality and non-discrimination as an important part of the foundation on which the entire structure of US-Soviet relations is built. An increase in the scale of commercial and economic ties corresponding to the potentials of both countries will cement this foundation and benefit the American and Soviet peoples.

The two Sides noted with satisfaction that since the previous summit meeting US-Soviet commercial and economic relations have on the whole shown an upward trend. This was expressed, in particular, in a substantial growth of the exchange of goods between the two countries which approximated $1.5 billion in 1973. It was noted that prospects were favorable for surpassing the goal announced in the joint US–USSR communiqué of June 24, 1973, of achieving a total bilateral trade turnover of $2–3 billion during the three-year period 1973–1975. The Joint US–USSR Commercial Commission continues to provide an effective mechanism to promote the broad-scale growth of economic relations.

The two Sides noted certain progress in the development of long-term cooperation between American firms and Soviet organizations in carrying out large-scale projects including those on a compensation basis. They are convinced that such cooperation is an important element in the development of commercial and economic ties between the two countries. The two Sides agreed to encourage the conclusion and implementation of appropriate agreements between American and Soviet organizations and firms. Taking into account the progress made in a number of specific projects, such as those concerning truck manufacture, the trade center, and chemical fertilizers, the Sides noted the possibility of concluding appropriate contracts in other areas of mutual interest, such as pulp and paper, timber, ferrous and nonferrous metallurgy, natural gas, the engineering industry, and the extraction and processing of high energy–consuming minerals.

Both Sides noted further development of productive contacts and ties between business circles of the two countries in which a positive role was played by the decisions taken during the previous summit meeting on the opening of a United States commercial office in Moscow and a USSR trade representation in Washington as well as the establishment of a US-Soviet Commercial and Economic Council. They expressed their desire to continue to bring about favorable conditions for the successful development of commercial and economic relations between the USA and the USSR.

Both Sides confirmed their interest in bringing into force at the earliest possible time the US-Soviet trade agreement of October 1972.

Desirous of promoting the further expansion of economic relations between the two countries, the two Sides signed a Long-Term Agreement to Facilitate Economic, Industrial and Technical Cooperation between the USA and the USSR. They believe that a consistent implementation of the cooperation embodied in the Agreement over the ten-year period will be an important factor in strengthening bilateral relations in general and will benefit the peoples of both countries.

Having reviewed the progress in carrying out the Agreement Regarding Certain Maritime Matters concluded in October 1972 for a period of three years, and based on the experience accumulated thus far, the two Sides expressed themselves in favor of concluding before its expiration a new agreement in this field. Negotiations concerning such an agreement will commence this year.

V. PROGRESS IN OTHER FIELDS OF BILATERAL RELATIONS

Having reviewed the progress in the implementation of the cooperative agreements concluded in 1972–1973, both Sides noted the useful work done by joint American-Soviet committees and working groups established under those agreements in developing regular contacts and cooperation between scientific and technical organizations, scientists, specialists and cultural personnel of both countries.

The two Sides note with satisfaction that joint efforts by the USA and the USSR in such fields of cooperation as medical science and public health, protection and improvement of man's environment, science and technology, exploration of outer space and the world ocean, peaceful uses of atomic energy, agriculture and transportation create conditions for an accelerated solution of some urgent and complicated problems facing mankind.

Such cooperation makes a substantial contribution to the development of the structure of American-Soviet relations, giving it a more concrete positive content.

Both Sides will strive to broaden and deepen their cooperation in science and technology as well as cultural exchanges on the basis of agreements concluded between them.

On the basis of positive experience accumulated in their scientific and technological cooperation and guided by the desire to ensure further progress in this important sphere of their mutual relations, the two Sides decided to extend such cooperation to the following new areas.

Energy

Taking into consideration the growing energy needs of industry, transportation and other branches of the economies of both countries and the consequent need to intensify scientific and technical cooperation in the development of optimal methods of utilizing traditional and new sources of energy, and to improve the understanding of the energy programs and problems of both countries, the two Sides concluded an agreement on cooperation in the field of energy. Responsibility for the implementation of the Agreement is entrusted to a US–USSR Joint Committee on Cooperation in Energy, which will be established for that purpose.

Housing and Other Construction

The two Sides signed an agreement on cooperation in the field of housing and other construction. The aim of this Agreement is to promote the solution by joint effort of problems related to modern techniques of housing and other construction along such lines as the improvement of the reliability and quality of buildings and building materials, the planning and construction of new towns, construction in seismic areas and areas of extreme climatic conditions. For the implementation of this Agreement there will be established a Joint US–USSR Committee on Cooperation in Housing and Other Construction which will determine specific working programs.

For the purpose of enhancing the safety of their peoples living in earthquake-prone areas, the two Sides agreed to undertake on a priority basis a joint research project to increase the safety of buildings and other structures in these areas and, in particular, to study the behavior of pre-fabricated residential structures during earthquakes.

Artificial Heart Research

In the course of the implementation of joint programs in the field of medical science and public health scientists and specialists of both countries concluded that there is a need to concentrate their efforts on the solution of one of the most important and humane problems of modern medical science, development of an artificial heart. In view of the great theoretical and technical complexity of the work involved, the two Sides concluded a special agreement on the subject. The US–USSR Joint Committee for Health Cooperation will assume responsibility for this project.

Cooperation in Space

The two Sides expressed their satisfaction with the successful preparations for the first joint manned flight of the American and Soviet spacecraft, Apollo and Soyuz, which is scheduled for 1975 and envisages their docking and mutual visits of the astronauts in each other's spacecraft. In accordance with existing agreements fruitful cooperation is being carried out in a number of other fields related to the exploration of outer space.

Attaching great importance to further American-Soviet cooperation in the exploration and use of outer space for peaceful purposes, including the development of safety systems for manned flights in space, and considering the desirability of consolidating experience in this field, the two Sides agreed to continue to explore possibilities for further joint space projects following the US–USSR space flight now scheduled for July 1975.

Transport of the Future

Aware of the importance of developing advanced modes of transportation, both Sides agreed that high-speed ground systems of the future, including a magnetically levitated train, which can provide economical, efficient, and reliable forms of transportation, would be a desirable and innovative area for joint activity. A working group to develop a joint research cooperation program in this area under the 1973 Agreement on Cooperation in the Field of Transportation will be established at the Fall meeting of the Joint US–USSR Transportation Committee.

Environmental Protection

Desiring to expand cooperation in the field of environmental protection, which is being successfully carried out under the US–USSR Agreement signed on May 23, 1972, and to contribute to the implementation of the "Man and the Biosphere" international program conducted on the initiative of the United Nations Educational, Scientific and Cultural Organization (UNESCO), both Sides agreed to designate in the territories of their respective countries certain natural areas as biosphere reserves for protecting valuable plant and animal genetic strains and ecosystems, and for conducting scientific research needed for more effective actions concerned with global environmental protection. Appropriate work for the implementation of this undertaking will be conducted in conformity with the goals of the UNESCO program and under the auspices of the previously established US–USSR Joint Committee on Cooperation in the Field of Environmental Protection.

Cultural Exchanges

The two Parties, aware of the importance of cultural exchanges as a means of promoting mutual understanding, express satisfaction with the agreement between the Metropolitan Museum of Art of New York City and the Ministry of Culture of the USSR leading to a major exchange of works of art. Such an exchange would be in accordance with the General Agreement on Contacts, Exchanges and Cooperation signed June 19, 1973, under which the parties agree to render assistance for the exchange of exhibitions between the museums of the two countries.

Establishment of New Consulates

Taking into consideration the intensive development of ties between the US and the USSR and the importance of further expanding consular relations on the basis of the US–USSR Consular Convention, and desiring to promote trade, tourism and cooperation between them in various areas, both Sides agreed to open additional Consulates General in two or three cities of each country.

As a first step they agreed in principle to the simultaneous establishment of a United States Consulate General in Kiev and a USSR Consulate General in New York. Negotiations for implementation of this agreement will take place at an early date.

*   *   *

Both Sides highly appreciate the frank and constructive atmosphere and fruitful results of the talks held between them in the course of the present meeting. They are convinced that the results represent a new and important milestone along the road of improving relations between the USA and the USSR to the benefit of the peoples of both countries, and a significant contribution to their efforts aimed at strengthening world peace and security.

Having again noted in this connection the exceptional importance and great practical usefulness of US-Soviet summit meetings, both Sides reaffirmed their agreement to hold such meetings regularly and when considered necessary for the discussion and solution of urgent questions. Both Sides also expressed their readiness to continue their active and close contacts and consultations.

The President extended an invitation to General Secretary of the Central Committee of the CPSU, L. I. Brezhnev, to pay an official visit to the United States in 1975. This invitation was accepted with pleasure.

July 3, 1974

For the United States of America:

For the Union of Soviet Socialist Republics:

RICHARD NIXON

L. BREZHNEV

President of the United States of America

General Secretary of the Central Committee of the CPSU

9. The Vladivostok Meetings:
23–24 November 1974

Initiation   Agreement at Moscow summit in June to hold "mini-summit" on offensive strategic missiles before the end of the year.

Itinerary   President Ford's state visit to Japan (November 18–22) and Korea (November 22–23).

Rationale   Reaffirm continuity in U.S. position on cooperative ties and SALT process.

Principals
  U.S.:   President Ford, Secretary of State and A/NSA Kissinger, Ambassador Stoessel, Assistant Secretary of State Hartman, Deputy A/NSA Lieutenant General Scowcroft; State Department: William Hyland and Helmut Sonnenfeldt.
  USSR: General Secretary Brezhnev, Foreign Minister Gromyko, Ambassador Dobrynin, Assistant to General Secretary Aleksandrov, Collegium of Ministry of Foreign Affairs member Korniyenko; Colonel General Kozlov (Main Operations Directorate of the General Staff).

Background   Resignation of President Nixon in the wake of Watergate in August 1974. Impasse on SALT II negotiations.

Preparation   Visit by Kissinger party to Moscow October 23–27, 1974. Strategic debate between Kissinger and Defense Secretary Schlesinger.

Discussions   Businesslike and constructive.

Issues   Reaffirmation of importance of strategic arms limitations and intention to conclude a new agreement in 1975; CSCE; mutual reduction of forces in Europe; Cyprus dispute; U.N. Resolution 338 and the Middle East; cooperative efforts.

Results   Joint Statement on Strategic Offensive Arms and Joint Communiqué, November 24th, agreeing to resumption of SALT negotiations in Geneva in January 1975 toward a new agreement to cover the period from October 1977 to December 31, 1985 covering ICBMs, SLBMs and MIRVs, and incorporating the Interim Agreement of May 26, 1972 which would remain in force until October 1977.

Also agreed to increasing the effectiveness of the Treaty on Non-Proliferation of Nuclear Weapons; negotiations on underground nuclear testing, environmental modification for military purposes and chemical warfare, and mutual force reductions in Central Europe.

Cyprus situation to be settled in accordance with U.N. measures.

Middle East still considered "dangerous situation" and efforts to be based on U.N. Resolution 338 and the Geneva Conference.

Continuation of broadening and deepening mutually advantageous cooperative commercial and economic projects, scientific, technical, and cultural ties.

Joint U.S.-Soviet Statement on Strategic Offensive Arms, Issued at Vladivostok, November 24, 1974[14]

During their working meeting in the area of Vladivostok on November 23–24, 1974, the President of the USA Gerald R. Ford and General Secretary of the Central Committee of the CPSU L. I. Brezhnev discussed in detail the question of further limitations of strategic offensive arms.

They reaffirmed the great significance that both the United States and the USSR attach to the limitation of strategic offensive arms. They are convinced that a long-term agreement on this question would be a significant contribution to improving relations between the US and the USSR, to reducing the danger of war and to enhancing world peace. Having noted the value of previous agreements on this question, including the Interim Agreement of May 26, 1972, they reaffirm the

---

[14]*Department of State Bulletin*, Vol. 71, No. 1852 (December 23, 1974), p. 879.

intention to conclude a new agreement on the limitation of strategic offensive arms, to last through 1985.

As a result of the exchange of views on the substance of such a new agreement, the President of the United States of America and the General Secretary of the Central Committee of the CPSU concluded that favorable prospects exist for completing the work on this agreement in 1975.

Agreement was reached that further negotiations will be based on the following provisions.

1. The new agreement will incorporate the relevant provisions of the Interim Agreement of May 26, 1972, which will remain in force until October 1977.

2. The new agreement will cover the period from October 1977 through December 31, 1985.

3. Based on the principle of equality and equal security, the new agreement will include the following limitations:

a. Both Sides will be entitled to have a certain agreed aggregate number of strategic delivery vehicles;

b. Both sides will be entitled to have a certain agreed aggregate number of ICBMs and SLBMs [intercontinental ballistic missiles; submarine-launched ballistic missiles] equipped with multiple independently targetable warheads (MIRVs).

4. The new agreement will include a provision for further negotiations beginning no later than 1980–1981 on the question of further limitations and possible reductions of strategic arms in the period after 1985.

5. Negotiations between the delegations of the U.S. and USSR to work out the new agreement incorporating the foregoing points will resume in Geneva in January 1975.

November 24, 1974.

Joint U.S.-Soviet Communiqué, Signed at Vladivostok, November 24, 1974[15]

In accordance with the previously announced agreement, a working meeting between the President of the United States of America Gerald R. Ford and the General Secretary of the Central Committee of the Communist Party of the Soviet Union L. I. Brezhnev took place in the area of Vladivostok on November 23 and 24, 1974. Taking part in the talks were the Secretary of State of the United States of America and Assistant to the President for National Security Affairs, Henry A. Kissinger, and Member of the Politburo of the Central Committee of the CPSU, Minister of Foreign Affairs of the USSR, A. A. Gromyko.

They discussed a broad range of questions dealing with American-Soviet relations and the current international situation.

Also taking part in the talks were:

On the American side Walter J. Stoessel, Jr., Ambassador of the USA to the USSR; Helmut Sonnenfeldt, Counselor of the Department of State; Arthur A. Hartman, Assistant Secretary of State for European Affairs; Lieutenant General Brent Scowcroft, Deputy Assistant to the President for National Security Affairs; and William Hyland, official of the Department of State.

On the Soviet side A. F. Dobrynin, Ambassador of the USSR to the USA; A. M. Aleksandrov, Assistant to the General Secretary of the Central Committee of the CPSU; and G. M. Korniyenko, Member of the Collegium of the Ministry of Foreign Affairs of the USSR.

I

The United States of America and the Soviet Union reaffirmed their determination to develop further their relations in the direction defined by the fundamental joint decisions and basic treaties and agreements concluded between the two Sides in recent years.

They are convinced that the course of American-Soviet relations, directed towards strengthening world peace, deepening the relaxation of international tensions and expanding mutually beneficial cooperation of states with different social systems meets the vital interests of the peoples of both States and other peoples.

---

[15]*Department of State Bulletin*, Vol. 71, No. 1852 (December 23, 1974), pp. 879–81.

Both Sides consider that based on the agreements reached between them important results have been achieved in fundamentally reshaping American-Soviet relations on the basis of peaceful coexistence and equal security. These results are a solid foundation for progress in reshaping Soviet-American relations.

Accordingly, they intend to continue, without a loss in momentum, to expand the scale and intensity of their cooperative efforts in all spheres as set forth in the agreements they have signed so that the process of improving relations between the US and the USSR will continue without interruption and will become irreversible.

Mutual determination was expressed to carry out strictly and fully the mutual obligations undertaken by the US and the USSR in accordance with the treaties and agreements concluded between them.

II

Special consideration was given in the course of the talks to a pivotal aspect of Soviet-American relations: measures to eliminate the threat of war and to halt the arms race.

Both Sides reaffirm that the Agreements reached between the US and the USSR on the prevention of nuclear war and the limitation of strategic arms are a good beginning in the process of creating guarantees against the outbreak of nuclear conflict and war in general. They expressed their deep belief in the necessity of promoting this process and expressed their hope that other states would contribute to it as well. For their part the US and the USSR will continue to exert vigorous efforts to achieve this historic task.

A joint statement on the question of limiting strategic offensive arms is being released separately.

Both sides stressed once again the importance and necessity of a serious effort aimed at preventing the dangers connected with the spread of nuclear weapons in the world. In this connection they stressed the importance of increasing the effectiveness of the Treaty on the Non-Proliferation of Nuclear Weapons.

It was noted that, in accordance with previous agreements, initial contacts were established between representatives of the US and of the USSR on questions related to underground nuclear explosions for peaceful purposes, to measures to overcome the dangers of the use of environmental modification techniques for military purposes, as well as measures dealing with the most dangerous lethal means of chemical warfare. It was agreed to continue an active search for mutually acceptable solutions of these questions.

III

In the course of the meeting an exchange of views was held on a number of international issues: special attention was given to negotiations already in progress in which the two Sides are participants and which are designed to remove existing sources of tension and to bring about the strengthening of international security and world peace.

Having reviewed the situation at the Conference on Security and Cooperation in Europe, both Sides concluded that there is a possibility for its early successful conclusion. They proceed from the assumption that the results achieved in the course of the Conference will permit its conclusion at the highest level and thus be commensurate with its importance in ensuring the peaceful future of Europe.

The USA and the USSR also attach high importance to the negotiations on mutual reduction of forces and armaments and associated measures in Central Europe. They agree to contribute actively to the search for mutually acceptable solutions on the basis of principle of undiminished security for any of the parties and the prevention of unilateral military advantages.

Having discussed the situation existing in the Eastern Mediterranean, both Sides state their firm support for the independence, sovereignty and territorial integrity of Cyprus and will make every effort in this direction. They consider that a just settlement of the Cyprus question must be based on the strict implementation of the resolutions adopted by the Security Council and the General Assembly of the United Nations regarding Cyprus.

In the course of the exchange of views on the Middle East both Sides expressed their concern with regard to the dangerous situation in that region. They reaffirmed their intention to make every effort to promote a solution of the key issues of a just and lasting peace in that area on the basis of the United Nations Resolution 338, taking into account the legitimate interests of all the peoples of the area, including the Palestinian people, and respect for the right to independent existence of all States in the area.

The Sides believe that the Geneva Conference should play an important part in the establishment of a just and lasting peace in the Middle East, and should resume its work as soon as possible.

IV

The state of relations was reviewed in the field of commercial, economic, scientific and technical ties between the USA and the USSR. Both Sides confirmed the great importance which further progress in these fields would have for Soviet-American relations, and expressed their firm intention to continue the broadening and deepening of mutually advantageous cooperation.

The two Sides emphasized the special importance accorded by them to the development on a long-term basis of commercial and economic cooperation, including mutually beneficial large-scale projects. They believe that such commercial and economic cooperation will serve the cause of increasing the stability of Soviet-American relations.

Both Sides noted with satisfaction the progress in the implementation of agreements and in the development of ties and cooperation between the US and the USSR in the fields of science, technology and culture. They are convinced that the continued expansion of such cooperation will benefit the peoples of both countries and will be an important contribution to the solution of world-wide scientific and technical problems.

The talks were held in an atmosphere of frankness and mutual understanding, reflecting the constructive desire of both Sides to strengthen and develop further the peaceful cooperative relationship between the USA and the USSR, and to ensure progress in the solution of outstanding international problems in the interests of preserving and strengthening peace.

The results of the talks provided a convincing demonstration of the practical value of Soviet-American summit meetings and their exceptional importance in the shaping of a new relationship between the United States of America and the Soviet Union.

President Ford reaffirmed the invitation to L. I. Brezhnev to pay an official visit to the United States in 1975. The exact date of the visit will be agreed upon later.

For the United States
of America:

For the Union of Soviet
Socialist Republics:

GERALD R. FORD

L. I. BREZHNEV

*President of the United
States of America*

*General Secretary
of the Central Committee
of the CPSU*

November 24, 1974

10. The Vienna Summit:
15–18 June 1979

Initiation   Explicitly linked to progress on SALT II agreement.

Rationale   Signature of SALT II Treaty.

Principals

U.S.:   President Carter, Secretary of State Vance, Secretary of
Defense Brown, A/NSA Brzezinski; General Jones,
Chairman, Joint Chiefs of Staff; ACDA Director Seig-
nious, Ambassador Toon, Presidential Assistants Jordan
and Powell; Ralph Earle, Chief of U.S. Delegation at
SALT talks.

USSR: General Secretary and President Brezhnev, Foreign
Minister Gromyko, Defense Minister Ustinov; Marshal
Ogarkov, Deputy Defense Minister and Chief of General
Staff; Secretary of Central Committee of CPSU Cher-
nenko; Assistant to General Secretary Aleksandrov,
Section Chief Zamyatin of Central Committee CPSU;
Deputy Foreign Minister Korniyenko, Ambassador
Dobrynin; Komplektov from Collegium; Karpov, Chief of
Soviet Delegation at SALT talks.

Background   Seven years of SALT negotiations under three presidents.
Failure of U.S. in Vietnam and collapse of Saigon in April
1975. Soviets cancel trade agreement in 1975, rejecting
Jackson-Vanik Amendment. Decline of détente; Soviet
moves in Angola, Horn of Africa. Chinese Vice Premier's
visit to Washington in January 1979 to normalize relations.

Preparation Secretary Vance's trip to Moscow in March 1977 for "deep
cuts" proves unproductive. President Carter's "three-tier"
approach; meetings with Gromyko and Dobrynin. Soviets
delay summit commitment until after completion of Deng
Xiaoping's visit to Washington. President's meeting with
Western allies in Guadeloupe (January 1979) to coordinate positions. Brezhnev agrees to summit early April
1979. Intensive personal preparations by the president.

Discussions Confirmed "specific significance" of personal and regular
meetings.

Issues SALT II Treaty, Reaffirmation of Basic Principles, Comprehensive Test Ban negotiations, importance of nuclear nonproliferation, Vienna negotiations on mutual force reductions in Central Europe, anti-satellite negotiations, limitation of conventional arms transfers, need to prepare proposals on chemical weapons prohibition and banning of radiological weapons, measures to limit arms in the Indian Ocean. International issues included endorsement of Final Act of CSCE and forthcoming Madrid All-European Conference in 1980, reaffirmation of peaceful settlement of Middle East problem, peaceful use of oceans and outer space, cooperative bilateral ties.

Results Joint communiqué of June 18th and signature of the following documents:
— Treaty on the Limitation of Strategic Offensive Arms, along with Agreed Statements and Common Understandings.
— Memorandum of Understanding regarding the Establishment of a Data Base on the Numbers of Strategic Offensive Arms.
— Joint Statement of Principles and Basic Guidelines for Subsequent Negotiations on the Limitation of Strategic Arms.
— Soviet Backfire Statement (limit production to 30 per year).

Joint U.S.-U.S.S.R. Communiqué, Vienna, June 18, 1979[16]

By mutual agreement, President of the United States of America Jimmy Carter and General Secretary of the CPSU [Communist Party of the Soviet Union] Central Committee and President of the Presidium of the USSR Supreme Soviet Leonid I. Brezhnev held meetings in Vienna, Austria, from June 15 to June 18, 1979. President Carter and President Brezhnev conducted their discussions with the participation of:

On the American side, Cyrus Vance, Secretary of State of the United States of America; Harold Brown, Secretary of Defense of the United States of America; Zbigniew Brzezinski, Assistant to the President for National Security Affairs; and General David Jones, Chairman of the Joint Chiefs of Staff.

On the Soviet side, A. A. Gromyko, Member of the Politburo of the CPSU and Minister of Foreign Affairs; D. F. Ustinov, Member of the Politburo of the CPSU and Minister of Defense; K. U. Chernenko, Member of the Politburo of the CPSU and Secretary of the Central Committee of the CPSU; and Marshal N. V. Ogarkov, First Deputy Minister of Defense of the USSR and Chief of the General Staff of the Armed Forces of the USSR.

Also participating in the talks were:

On the American side, George Seignious, Director of the Arms Control and Disarmament Agency; Hamilton Jordan, Assistant to the President; Jody Powell, Assistant to the President; Malcolm Toon, Ambassador of the United States of America to the USSR; and Ralph Earle, Chief of the US Delegation at the Strategic Arms Limitation Talks.

On the Soviet side, A. M. Aleksandrov, Assistant to the General Secretary of the Central Committee of the CPSU; L. M. Zamyatin, Section Chief of the Central Committee of the CPSU; G. M. Korniyenko, First Deputy Minister of Foreign Affairs of the USSR; A. F. Dobrynin, Ambassador of the USSR to the United States of America; V. G. Komplektov, Member of the Collegium of the Ministry of Foreign

---

[16]Department of State Selected Documents, No. 13, "Vienna Summit, June 15–18, 1979" (USGPO: 1979 0-296-125), pp. 6–8.

Affairs of the USSR; and V. P. Karpov, Chief of the USSR Delegation at the Strategic Arms Limitation Talks.

President Carter and President Brezhnev signed the Treaty on the Limitation of Strategic Offensive Arms. Basic issues of US-Soviet relations and pressing international problems were also discussed. The exchange of views was characterized by the desire to expand mutual understanding and to find mutually acceptable solutions to problems of interest to both sides. In their discussions they devoted special attention to reducing the risk of war through further limits on strategic arms and through other endeavors in arms limitation and disarmament.

The two sides expressed their appreciation to the Government of Austria for its hospitality and for providing all necessary facilities for the success of the meetings.

I. General Aspects of US-Soviet Relations

There is agreement between the sides that the state of relations between the United States and the Soviet Union is of great importance for the fundamental interests of the peoples of both countries and that it significantly affects the development of the international situation as a whole. Recognizing the great responsibility connected with this, the sides have expressed their firm intent to continue working toward the establishment of a more stable and constructive foundation for US-Soviet relations. To this end, the two sides acknowledged the necessity of expanding areas of cooperation between them.

Such cooperation should be based on the principles of complete equality, equal security, respect for sovereignty and non-intervention in each other's internal affairs, and should facilitate the relaxation of international tension and the peaceful conduct of mutually beneficial relations between states, and thereby enhance international stability and world peace.

The sides reaffirmed their conviction that full implementation of each of the provisions of the "Basic Principles of Relations between the United States of America and the Union of Soviet Socialist Republics" as well as other treaties and agreements concluded between them would contribute to a more stable relationship between the two countries.

The two sides stressed the importance of peaceful resolution of disputes, respect for the sovereignty and territorial integrity of states, and of efforts so that conflicts or situations would not arise which could serve to increase international tensions. They recognize the right of the

peoples of all states to determine their future without outside interference.

Recognizing that an armed world conflict can and must be avoided,
the sides believe that at the present time there is no more important and
urgent task for mankind than ending the arms race and preventing war.
They expressed their intention to make every effort to attain that goal.
To that end, they also recognized the value of consultation between
themselves and with other governments, at the United Nations and
elsewhere, in order to prevent and eliminate conflict in various regions
of the world.

The sides note with satisfaction the growing practice of contacts
between government officials of the USA and the USSR in the course of
which key questions of US-Soviet relations and pressing international
issues are discussed. The process of developing useful ties between the
US Congress and the Supreme Soviet of the USSR and of exchanges
between non-governmental organizations is continuing.

The talks again confirmed the specific significance of personal
meetings between the leaders of the USA and the USSR in resolving the
basic questions in the relations between the two states. In principle, it
has been agreed that such meetings will be held in the future on a
regular basis, with the understanding that the specific timing will be
determined by mutual agreement.

Agreement has also been reached on broadening the practice of
consultations and exchanges of opinion between representatives of the
sides on other levels.

II. Limitations of Nuclear and Conventional Arms

The two sides reaffirmed their deep conviction that special importance should be attached to the problems of the prevention of
nuclear war and to curbing the competition in strategic arms. Both sides
recognized that nuclear war would be a disaster for all mankind. Each
stated that it is not striving and will not strive for military superiority,
since that can only result in dangerous instability, generating higher
levels of armaments with no benefit to the security of either side.

Recognizing that the USA and the USSR have a special responsibility
to reduce the risk of nuclear war and contribute to world peace,
President Carter and President Brezhnev committed themselves to take
major steps to limit nuclear weapons with the objective of ultimately

eliminating them, and to complete successfully other arms limitation and disarmament negotiations.

SALT. In the course of the meeting, President Carter and President Brezhnev confirmed and signed the Treaty Between the USA and the USSR on the Limitation of Strategic Offensive Arms, the Protocol thereto, the Joint Statement of Principles and Basic Guidelines for Subsequent Negotiations on the Limitation of Strategic Arms and the document entitled Agreed Statements and Common Understandings Regarding the Treaty Between the USA and USSR on the Limitation of Strategic Offensive Arms.[17]

At the same time, the sides again stressed the great significance of the Treaty on the Limitation of Anti-Ballistic Missile Systems and strict compliance with its provisions and of other agreements previously concluded between them in the field of strategic arms limitations and reducing the danger of nuclear war.

Both sides express their deep satisfaction with the process of the negotiations on strategic arms limitations and the fact that their persistent efforts for many years to conclude a new treaty have been crowned with success. This treaty sets equal ceilings on the nuclear delivery systems of both sides; to begin the process of reductions it requires the reduction of existing nuclear arms; to begin to limit the threat represented by the qualitative arms race it also places substantial constraints on the modernization of strategic offensive systems and the development of new ones.

The new Treaty on the Limitation of Strategic Offensive Arms and the Protocol thereto represent a mutually acceptable balance between the interests of the sides based on the principles of equality and equal security. These documents are a substantial contribution to the prevention of nuclear war and the deepening of detente, and thus serve the interests not only of the American and Soviet peoples, but the aspirations of mankind for peace.

The two sides reaffirmed their commitment strictly to observe every provision in the treaty.

---

[17]The text of the SALT II Treaty and Protocol as signed in Vienna on June 18, 1979, and accompanying Agreed Statement and Common Understandings, can be found in *Arms Control and Disarmament Agreements: Texts and Histories of Negotiations* (Washington, DC: United States Arms Control and Disarmament Agency, 1982), pp. 246 ff.

President Carter and President Brezhnev discussed questions relating to the SALT III negotiations and in this connection expressed the firm intention of the sides to act in accordance with the Joint Statement of Principles and Basic Guidelines for Subsequent Negotiations on the Limitation of Strategic Arms.

Comprehensive Test Ban Treaty. It was noted that there has been definite progress at the negotiations, in which the UK is also participating, on an international treaty comprehensively banning test explosions of nuclear weapons in any environment and an associated protocol. They confirmed the intention of the USA and the USSR to work, together with the UK, to complete preparation of this treaty as soon as possible.

Non-proliferation. The two sides reaffirmed the importance they attach to nuclear non-proliferation. They consistently advocate the further strengthening of the regime of non-proliferation of nuclear weapons and confirm their resolve to continue to comply strictly with the obligations they have assumed under the Treaty on the Non-Proliferation of Nuclear Weapons. They stressed the importance of applying comprehensive international safeguards under the International Atomic Energy Agency and pledged to continue their efforts to strengthen these safeguards.

They noted the profound threat posed to world security by the proliferation of nuclear weapons, and agreed that the states already possessing nuclear weapons bear a special responsibility to demonstrate restraint. To this end, they affirmed their joint conviction that further efforts are needed, including on a regional basis, and expressed the hope that the conclusion of the SALT II Treaty will make an important contribution toward non-proliferation objectives.

Both sides further committed themselves to close cooperation, along with other countries, to insure a successful conclusion to the Non-Proliferation Treaty Review Conference in 1980, and called upon all states which have not already done so to sign and ratify the Non-Proliferation Treaty.

Vienna Negotiations. President Carter and President Brezhnev emphasized the great importance the sides attached to the negotiations on the mutual reduction of forces and armaments and associated measures in Central Europe in which they are participating with other states. A reduction of the military forces of both sides and the implementation of associated measures in Central Europe would be a major contribution to stability and security.

ASAT. It was also agreed to continue actively searching for mutually acceptable agreements in the ongoing negotiations on anti-satellite systems.

Conventional Arms Transfers. The two sides agreed that their respective representatives will meet promptly to discuss questions related to the next round of negotiations on limiting conventional arms transfers.

Chemical Weapons. The two sides reaffirmed the importance of a general, complete and verifiable prohibition of chemical weapons and agreed to intensify their efforts to prepare an agreed joint proposal for presentation to the Committee on Disarmaments.

Radiological Weapons. President Carter and President Brezhnev were pleased to be able to confirm that bilateral agreement on major elements of a treaty banning the development, production, stockpiling and use of radiological weapons has been reached. An agreed joint proposal will be presented to the Committee on Disarmament this year.

Indian Ocean. The two sides agreed that their respective representatives will meet promptly to discuss the resumption of the talks on questions concerning arms limitation measures in the Indian Ocean.

Other Questions of Arms Limitations and General Disarmament. In discussing other questions connected with solving the problems of limiting the arms race and of disarmament, the sides expressed their support for the Final Document adopted at the Special on Session of the UN General Assembly on Disarmament. The sides noted their support for a second special session of the UN General Assembly devoted to disarmament and for that session to be followed by the convocation of a World Disarmament Conference with universal participation, adequately prepared and at an appropriate time.

The USA and the USSR will continue to cooperate between themselves and with other member states of the Committee on Disarmament with its enlarged membership for the purpose of working out effective steps in the field of disarmament in that forum.

In summing up the exchange of views on the state of negotiations being conducted between the USA and the USSR, or with their participation, on a number of questions connected with arms limitation and disarmament, the sides agreed to give new impetus to the joint efforts to achieve practical results at these negotiations.

III. International Issues

There was a broad exchange of views on major international issues. The sides expressed their support for the process of international detente which in their view should become increasingly specific in nature and spread to all areas of the globe, thus helping to promote increased international stability.

President Carter and President Brezhnev devoted particular attention to situations of tension which complicate the international situation and interfere with positive developments in other areas. The two sides believe that all states must conduct themselves with particular responsibility and restraint in order to contribute to the elimination of present situations of tension and to prevent new ones from arising.

The two sides noted the importance of increasing international cooperation on such global issues as the promotion of worldwide economic development, the protection of the environment, and the peaceful use of space and the world ocean for the benefit of all mankind. They expressed their support for the efforts of the developing countries to deal with the problems they face.

Noting the important role of the UN as an instrument for maintaining peace, security and the development of international cooperation, the USA and the USSR confirm their intention to promote the improvement of the effectiveness of this organization on the basis of the UN Charter.

The sides noted with satisfaction the positive developments which have taken place in recent years with respect to the situation on the European continent. They underscored the significance of the Final Act of the Conference on Security and Cooperation in Europe. The two sides agreed that continuation of the CSCE process is important to promote security and cooperation in Europe. They called attention to the need for full implementation of all the provisions of the Helsinki Final Act. The USA and the USSR will work to facilitate a constructive meeting of the representatives of the participating states of the All-European Conference, which is scheduled to take place in 1980 in Madrid.

Each side reaffirmed its interest in a just, comprehensive and lasting peace in the Middle East and set forth its position on ways and means of resolving the Middle East problem.

There was an exchange of views concerning developments in Africa. They noted some normalization of the situation in certain areas of that continent, and the efforts of the independent states of Africa toward cooperation, economic development and peaceful relations and the positive role in this respect of the Organization of African Unity. They also indicated their respective views regarding the situation in Southern Africa.

The sides recognized the importance to world peace of peace and stability in Asia. They agreed that the independence, sovereignty and territorial integrity of all nations in the area must be fully respected. They also indicated their respective views regarding the situation in Southeast Asia.

IV. Cooperation in Bilateral Matters

The importance of cooperation between the USA and the USSR on the basis of mutual benefit, in accordance with the agreements which exist between the two countries, was emphasized. The sides took note of positive developments in the wide range of cultural, academic, scientific and technical exchange programs, which are continuing between the two countries.

Proceeding on the established principles of equality, reciprocity and mutual benefit as the basis for the conduct of such programs, the sides reaffirmed their commitment to continue and intensify cooperation in these areas.

The two sides confirmed that economic and commercial relations represent an important element in the development of improved bilateral ties. Both sides stated their position in favor of strengthening these relations, and recognized the necessity of working toward the elimination of obstacles to mutually beneficial trade and financial relations. The two sides expressed their determination to encourage the relevant organizations and enterprises in their respective countries to enter into mutually beneficial commercial agreements and contracts on a long-term basis.

President Carter and President Brezhnev expressed mutual satisfaction with the results of the talks which were held. They are convinced that the deepening of mutual understanding between the sides on several issues as a result of the meeting and the consistent implementation of the agreements which have been reached will facilitate the development of US-Soviet relations and represents a joint contribution of the two countries to strengthening detente, international security and peace.

JIMMY CARTER
President of the
United States of America

L. BREZHNEV
General Secretary, CC CPSU
President of the Presidium of
the Supreme Soviet of the USSR

June 18, 1979

11. The Geneva Summit:
19–21 November 1985

Initiation   Personal message from President Reagan conveyed by Vice President Bush after funeral ceremonies for General Secretary Chernenko.

Rationale   A "fresh start" to arrest and reverse the decline in relations.

Principals

U.S.:   President Reagan, Secretary of State Shultz, Chief of Staff Regan, A/NSA McFarlane, Ambassador to the U.S.S.R. Hartman, Special Advisor for Arms Control Nitze, Assistant Secretary of State for European Affairs Ridgway, Special Assistant for National Security Affairs Matlock.

USSR: General Secretary Gorbachev, Minister of Foreign Affairs Shevardnadze, First Deputy Foreign Minister Korniyenko, Ambassador Dobrynin, Head of Department of Propaganda Yakovlev, Head of Department of International Information Zamyatin, Assistant to the General Secretary Aleksandrov.

Background   Soviet invasion of Afghanistan in December 1979 resulting in U.S. grain embargo and abandonment of SALT II ratification efforts in U.S. Senate. Rise of American conservatism and anti-Soviet rhetoric. Start of intermediate nuclear forces (INF) talks in November 1981. Martial law imposed in Poland in December 1981, followed by U.S. efforts to boycott Soviet natural gas pipeline to Western Europe. These efforts end November 1982 after Andropov succeeds Brezhnev. Space-based missile defense concept (Strategic Defense Initiative, SDI) unveiled by Reagan in March 1983. Soviets shoot down KAL Flight 007 over Sea of Japan in September 1983. Start of planned deployment of cruise and Pershing II missiles in Western Europe in November 1983 prompts Soviet walkout from arms talks in Geneva. Chernenko succeeds Andropov in February 1984. Soviet boycott of 1984 Olympics in Los Angeles. Reagan-Gromyko talks in September 1984. Shultz and Gromyko meet in January

1985 and agree to resumpton of arms talks. Chernenko's death on March 10, 1985.

Preparation After lengthy delay following President Reagan's invitation, agreement reached on July 2, 1985 on date and location for meeting. Shultz meets with new Foreign Minister Shevardnadze at end of July in Helsinki for preliminary discussions on agenda. In September Shevardnadze meets with Shultz and McFarlane in New York and with Reagan and others in Washington. Shultz and party visit Moscow November 4–5 for more detailed talks with Gorbachev and Shevardnadze; "deep differences" remain, prospects for summit bleak.

Discussions Frank and useful but mutual acknowledgement that serious differences remain on a number of critical issues; 15 hours of meetings, including 5 hours of private discussions.

Issues Strategic Defense Initiative and its relation to possible agreement on 50 percent reduction in nuclear arms. Separation of INF negotiations from strategic arms discussions. Nuclear nonproliferation and chemical weapons. Regional conflict: Afghanistan, Angola, Ethiopia, Kampuchea, El Salvador, Nicaragua. Bilateral relations: cultural exchanges, consulates in Kiev and New York City, air travel. Human rights.

Results Joint Statement issued November 21, 1985. Signature by Shultz and Shevardnadze of Agreement on Contacts and Exchanges in Scientific, Educational and Cultural Fields.

Additional summit meetings agreed upon: Gorbachev to visit U.S. as early as June 1986; Reagan to visit Moscow in 1987. Secretary Shultz and Foreign Minister Shevardnadze to hold regular meetings.

No movement on SDI or Soviet heavy offensive missiles. Agreed to accelerate negotiations on strategic arms and called for "early progress" in areas where there is common ground, including "the principle of 50 percent reductions." Agreed to negotiate a separate interim INF agreement.

Agreed nuclear wars cannot be won; neither side to pursue military superiority; need to prevent an arms race in space; reaffirmed intentions to strengthen nuclear nonproliferation, to reach agreement to end chemical weapons, and to study the feasibility of risk reduction centers. Supported the need to give concrete expression to confidence- and security-building measures.

Agreed on the opening of consulates in Kiev and New York City "at an early date"; air safety measures in the North Pacific; the resumption of air services; and consultation on cooperative measures for environmental protection.

No statement on specific human rights or regional issues.

Joint Statement, Geneva, November 21, 1985[18]

By mutual agreement, President of the United States Ronald Reagan and General Secretary of the Central Committee of the Communist Party of the Soviet Union Mikhail Gorbachev met in Geneva November 19–21. Attending the meeting on the U.S. side were Secretary of State George Shultz; Chief of Staff Donald Regan; Assistant to the President Robert McFarlane; Ambassador to the USSR Arthur Hartman; Special Advisor to the President and the Secretary of State for Arms Control Paul H. Nitze; Assistant Secretary of State for European Affairs Rozanne Ridgway; Special Assistant to the President for National Security Affairs Jack Matlock. Attending on the Soviet side were Member of the Politburo of the Central Committee of the CPSU, Minister of Foreign Affairs E.A. Shevardnadze; First Deputy Foreign Minister G. M. Korniyenko; Ambassador to the United States A. F. Dobrynin; Head of the Department of Propaganda of the Central Committee of the CPSU, A. N. Yakovlev; Head of the Department of International Information of the Central Committee of the CPSU, L. M.

---

[18]*Weekly Compilation of Presidential Documents*, 21:47 (November 25, 1985), 1421–22.

Zamyatin; Assistant to the General Secretary of the Central Committee of the CPSU, A. M. Aleksandrov.

These comprehensive discussions covered the basic questions of U.S.-Soviet relations and the current international situation. The meetings were frank and useful. Serious differences remain on a number of critical issues.

While acknowledging the differences in their systems and approaches to international issues, some greater understanding of each side's view was achieved by the two leaders. They agreed about the need to improve U.S.-Soviet relations and the international situation as a whole.

In this connection the two sides have confirmed the importance of an ongoing dialogue, reflecting their strong desire to seek common ground on existing problems.

They agreed to meet again in the nearest future. The General Secretary accepted an invitation by the President of the United States to visit the United States of America and the President of the United States accepted an invitation by the General Secretary of the Central Committee of the CPSU to visit the Soviet Union. Arrangements for and timing of the visits will be agreed upon through diplomatic channels.

In their meetings, agreement was reached on a number of specific issues. Areas of agreement are registered on the following pages.

SECURITY

The sides, having discussed key security issues, and conscious of the special responsibility of the USSR and the U.S. for maintaining peace, have agreed that a nuclear war cannot be won and must never be fought. Recognizing that any conflict between the USSR and the U.S. could have catastrophic consequences, they emphasized the importance of preventing any war between them, whether nuclear or conventional. They will not seek to achieve military superiority.

NUCLEAR AND SPACE TALKS

The President and the General Secretary discussed the negotiations on nuclear and space arms.

They agreed to accelerate the work at these negotiations, with a view to accomplishing the tasks set down in the Joint U.S.-Soviet Agreement of January 8, 1985, namely to prevent an arms race in space and to terminate it on earth, to limit and reduce nuclear arms and enhance strategic stability.

Noting the proposals recently tabled by the U.S. and the Soviet

Union, they called for early progress, in particular in areas where there is common ground, including the principle of 50% reductions in the nuclear arms of the U.S. and the USSR appropriately applied, as well as the idea of an interim INF agreement.

During the negotiation of these agreements, effective measures for verification of compliance with obligations assumed will be agreed upon.

RISK REDUCTION CENTERS

The sides agreed to study the question at the expert level of centers to reduce nuclear risk taking into account the issues and developments in the Geneva negotiations. They took satisfaction in such recent steps in this direction as the modernization of the Soviet-U.S. hotline.

NUCLEAR NON-PROLIFERATION

General Secretary Gorbachev and President Reagan reaffirmed the commitment of the USSR and the U.S. to the Treaty on the Non-Proliferation of Nuclear Weapons and their interest in strengthening together with other countries the non-proliferation regime, and in further enhancing the effectiveness of the Treaty, *inter alia* by enlarging its membership.

They note with satisfaction the overall positive results of the recent Review Conference of the Treaty on the Non-Proliferation of Nuclear Weapons.

The USSR and the U.S. reaffirm their commitment, assumed by them under the Treaty on the Non-Proliferation of Nuclear Weapons, to pursue negotiations in good faith on matters of nuclear arms limitation and disarmament in accordance with Article VI of the Treaty.

The two sides plan to continue to promote the strengthening of the International Atomic Energy Agency and to support the activities of the Agency in implementing safeguards as well as in promoting the peaceful uses of nuclear energy.

They view positively the practice of regular Soviet-U.S. consultations on non-proliferation of nuclear weapons which have been businesslike and constructive and express their intent to continue this practice in the future.

CHEMICAL WEAPONS

In the context of disussing security problems, the two sides reaffirmed that they are in favor of a general and complete prohibition of chemical weapons and the destruction of existing stockpiles of such weapons. They agreed to accelerate efforts to conclude an effective and verifiable international convention on this matter.

The two sides agreed to intensify bilateral discussions on the level of experts on all aspects of such a chemical weapons ban, including the question of verification. They agreed to initiate a dialogue on preventing the proliferation of chemical weapons.

MBFR

The two sides emphasized the importance they attach to the Vienna (MBFR) negotiations and expressed their willingness to work for positive results.

CDE

Attaching great importance to the Stockholm Conference on Confidence and Security Building Measures and Disarmament in Europe and noting the progress made there, the two sides stated their intention to facilitate, together with the other participating states, an early and successful completion of the work of the conference. To this end, they reaffirmed the need for a document which would include mutually acceptable confidence and security building measures and give concrete expression and effect to the principle of non-use of force.

PROCESS OF DIALOGUE

President Reagan and General Secretary Gorbachev agreed on the need to place on a regular basis and intensify dialogue at various levels. Along with meetings between the leaders of the two countries, this envisages regular meetings between the USSR Minister of Foreign Affairs and the U.S. Secretary of State, as well as between the heads of other Ministries and Agencies. They agree that the recent visits of the heads of Ministries and Departments in such fields as agriculture, housing and protection of the environment have been useful.

Recognizing that exchanges of views on regional issues on the expert level have proven useful, they agreed to continue such exchanges on a regular basis.

The sides intend to expand the programs of bilateral cultural, educational and scientific-technical exchanges, and also to develop trade and economic ties. The President of the United States and the

General Secretary of the Central Committee of the CPSU attended the signing of the Agreement on Contacts and Exchanges in Scientific, Educational and Cultural Fields.

They agreed on the importance of resolving humanitarian cases in the spirit of cooperation.

They believe that there should be greater understanding among our peoples and that to this end they will encourage greater travel and people-to-people contact.

NORTHERN PACIFIC AIR SAFETY

The two leaders also noted with satifaction that, in cooperation with the Government of Japan, the United States and the Soviet Union have agreed to a set of measures to promote safety on air routes in the North Pacific and have worked out steps to implement them.

CIVIL AVIATION/CONSULATES

They acknowledged that delegations from the United States and the Soviet Union have begun negotiations aimed at resumption of air services. The two leaders expressed their desire to reach a mutually beneficial agreement at an early date. In this regard, an agreement was reached on the simultaneous opening of Consulates General in New York and Kiev.

ENVIRONMENTAL PROTECTION

Both sides agreed to contribute to the preservation of the environment—a global task—through joint research and practical measures. In accordance with the existing U.S.-Soviet agreement in this area, consultations will be held next year in Moscow and Washington on specific programs of cooperation.

EXCHANGE INITIATIVES

The two leaders agreed on the utility of broadening exchanges and contacts including some of their new forms in a number of scientific, educational, medical and sports fields (*inter alia*, cooperation in the development of educational exchanges and software for elementary and secondary school instruction; measures to promote Russian language studies in the United States and English language studies in the USSR; the annual exchange of professors to conduct special courses in history, culture and economics at the relevant departments of Soviet and

American institutions of higher education; mutual allocation of scholarships for the best students in the natural sciences, technology, social sciences and humanities for the period of an academic year; holding regular meets in various sports and increased television coverage of sports events). The two sides agreed to resume cooperation in combatting cancer diseases.

The relevant agencies in each of the countries are being instructed to develop specific programs for these exchanges. The resulting programs will be reviewed by the leaders at their next meeting.

FUSION RESEARCH

The two leaders emphasized the potential importance of the work aimed at utilizing controlled thermonuclear fusion for peaceful purposes and, in this connection, advocated the widest practicable development of international cooperation in obtaining this source of energy, which is essentially inexhaustible, for the benefit for all mankind.

Remarks on Issuing a Joint Statement, Geneva, November 21, 1985[19]

General Secretary Gorbachev. You've already been handed the joint statement. The President and I have done a huge amount of work. We've gone into great detail; we've really done it in depth. And we've done it totally openly and frankly. We've discussed several most important isues. The relations between our two countries and the situation in the world in general today—these are issues and problems the solving of which in the most concrete way is of concern both to our countries and to the peoples of other countries in the world.

We discussed these issues basing our discussions on both sides' determination to improve relations between the Soviet Union and the United States of America. We decided that we must help to decrease the threat of nuclear war. We must not allow the arms race to move off into space, and we must cut it down on Earth.

It goes without saying that discussions of these sorts we consider to be

---

[19]*Weekly Compilation of Presidential Documents*, 21:47 (November 25, 1985), 1422-24.

very useful, and in its results you find a clear reflection of what the two sides have agreed together. We have to be realistic and straightforward and, therefore, the solving of the most important problems concerning the arms race and increasing hopes of peace, we didn't succeed in reaching at this meeting.

So, of course there are important disagreements on matters of principle that remain between us; however, the President and I have agreed that this work of seeking mutually acceptable decisions for these questions will be continued here in Geneva by our representatives. We're also going to seek new kinds of developing bilateral Soviet-American relations. And also we're going to have further consultations on several important questions where, for the most part, our positions, again, are completely different. All this [sic], we consider these forthcoming talks to be very, very useful.

But the significance of everything which we have agreed with the President can only, of course, be reflected if we carry it on into concrete measures. If we really want to succeed in something, then both sides are going to have to do an awful lot of work in the spirit of the joint statement which we have put out. And in this connection, I would like to announce that the Soviet Union, for its part, will do all it can in this cooperation with the United States of America in order to achieve practical results to cut down the arms race, to cut down the arsenals which we've piled up, and produce the conditions which will be necessary for peace on Earth and in space.

We make this announcement perfectly aware of our responsibility both to our own people and to the other peoples of the Earth. And we would very much hope that we can have the same approach from the administration of the United States of America. If that can be so, then, the work that has been done in these days in Geneva will not have been done in vain.

I would like to finish by thanking most profoundly the Government of Switzerland for the conditions which they've created for us to be able to work.

The President. President Furgler, General Secretary Gorbachev, may I express Nancy's and my deep personal appreciation and that of all Americans to the people of Switzerland for welcoming us so warmly and preparing the foundations for productive discussions. Yours is a long and honorable tradition of promoting international peace and understanding. You should take pride in being the capital for international discussions. So, again, to the Government of Switzerland and to the citizens of Geneva, many, many thanks.

We've packed a lot into the last 2 days. I came to Geneva to seek a fresh start in relations between the United States and the Soviet Union, and we have done this. General Secretary Gorbachev and I have held comprehensive disussions covering all elements of our relationship. I'm convinced that we are heading in the right direction. We've reached some useful interim results which are described in the joint statement that is being issued this morning.

In agreeing to accelerate the work of our nuclear arms negotiators, Mr. Gorbachev and I have addressed our common responsibility to strengthen peace. I believe that we have established a process for more intensive contacts between the United States and the Soviet Union. These 2 days of talks should inject a certain momentum into our work on the issues between us, a momentum we can continue at the meeting that we have agreed on for the next year.

Before coming to Geneva, I spoke often of the need to build confidence in our dealings with each other. Frank and forthright conversation at the summit are part of this process, but I'm certain General Secretary Gorbachev would agree that real confidence in each other must be built on deeds, not simply words. This is the thought that ties together all the proposals that the United States has put on the table in the past, and this is the criteria by which our meetings will be judged in the future.

The real report card on Geneva will not come in for months or even years, but we know the questions that must be answered. Will we join together in sharply reducing offensive nuclear arms and moving to nonnuclear defensive strengths for systems to make this a safer world? Will we join together to help bring about a peaceful resolution of conflicts in Asia, Africa, and Central America so that the peoples there can freely determine their own destiny without outside interference? Will the cause of liberty be advanced, and will the treaties and agreements signed—past and future—be fulfilled? The people of America, the Soviet Union, and throughout the world are ready to answer yes.

I leave Geneva today and our fireside summit determined to pursue every opportunity to build a safer world of peace and freedom. There's hard work ahead, but we're ready for it. General Secretary Gorbachev, we ask you to join us in getting the job done, as I'm sure you will.

Thank you.

Select Bibliography

Beam, Jacob. *Multiple Exposure: An American Ambassador's Unique Perspective on East-West Issues.* New York: W.W. Norton & Co., 1978.

Bohlen, Charles E. *Witness to History 1929–1969.* New York: W.W. Norton & Co., 1973.

Brzezinski, Zbigniew. *Power and Principle: Memoirs of the National Security Adviser, 1977–1981.* New York: Farrar, Straus and Giroux, 1983.

Carter, Jimmy. *Keeping Faith: Memoirs of a President.* New York: Bantam Books, 1982.

Eisenhower, Dwight D. *The White House Years: Mandate for Change, 1953–1956.* Garden City, New York: Doubleday & Co., 1963.

_____. *The White House Years: Waging Peace, 1956–1961.* Garden City, New York: Doubleday & Co., 1965.

Eubank, Keith. *The Summit Conferences 1919–1960.* Norman, Oklahoma: The University of Oklahoma Press, 1966.

Ford, Gerald R. *A Time to Heal.* New York: Harper & Row, 1979.

Garthoff, Raymond L. *Détente and Confrontation: American-Soviet Relations from Nixon to Reagan.* Washington, D.C.: The Brookings Institution, 1985.

_____. "Negotiating SALT." *The Wilson Quarterly,* Autumn 1977.

_____. "Negotiating with the Russians: Some Lessons from SALT." *International Security* 1:4 (Spring 1977).

George, Alexander L. *Managing U.S.-Soviet Rivalry: Problems of Crisis Prevention.* Boulder, Colorado: Westview Press, 1963.

Griffith, Robert, ed. *Ike's Letters to a Friend, 1941–1958.* Lawrence, Kansas: University Press of Kansas, 1984.

Hilsman, Roger. *To Move a Nation.* Garden City, New York: Doubleday & Co., 1967.

Hughes, Emmet John. *The Ordeal of Power*. New York: Atheneum, 1963.

Johnson, Lyndon Baines. *The Vantage Point: Perspectives of the Presidency 1963-1969*. New York: Holt, Rinehart, and Winston, 1971.

Khrushchev, Nikita. *Khrushchev Remembers*. Introduction, Commentary and Notes by Edward Crankshaw. Translated and edited by Strobe Talbott. Boston: Little, Brown and Co., 1970.

_____. *Khrushchev Remembers: The Last Testament*. Translated and edited by Strobe Talbott. Boston: Little, Brown and Co., 1974.

Kissinger, Henry A. *White House Years*. Boston: Little, Brown and Co., 1979.

_____. *Years of Upheaval*. Boston: Little, Brown and Co., 1982.

Nixon, Richard M. *RN, The Memoirs of Richard Nixon*. New York: Grosset & Dunlap, 1978.

Nye, Joseph S., Jr., ed. *The Making of America's Soviet Policy*. A Council on Foreign Relations Book. New Haven: Yale University Press, 1984.

Plischke, Elmer, ed. *Modern Diplomacy: The Art and the Artisans*. Washington, D.C.: American Enterprise Institute for Public Policy Research, 1979.

_____. *Summit Diplomacy: Personal Diplomacy of the President of the United States*. College Park, Maryland: University of Maryland, 1958.

Rostow, W.W. *The Diffusion of Power*. New York: The Macmillan Co., 1972.

_____. *Open Skies (Eisenhower's Proposal of July 21, 1955)*. Austin: University of Texas Press, 1982.

_____. *The United States in the World Arena*. New York: Harper & Row, 1960.

Schlesinger, Arthur M., Jr. *A Thousand Days: John F. Kennedy in the White House*. Boston: Houghton Mifflin, The Riverside Press, Cambridge, 1965.

Simes, Dimitri K. *Détente and Conflict in Soviet Foreign Policy 1972-1977*. The Washington Papers, vol. V, no. 44. Washington, D.C.: Center for Strategic and International Studies, Georgetown University, 1977.

Shevchenko, Arkady N. *Breaking with Moscow*. New York: Alfred A. Knopf, 1985.

Sorenson, Theodore C. *Kennedy*. New York: Harper & Row, 1965.

Talbott, Strobe. *Deadly Gambits: The Reagan Administration and the Stalemate in Nuclear Arms Control.* New York: Alfred A. Knopf, 1984.

————. *Endgame: The Inside Story of SALT II.* New York: Harper & Row, 1979.

U.S. Congress, House, Committee on Foreign Affairs (96th Congress, 1st Session). Special Study Series on Foreign Affairs Issues, Vol I. *Soviet Diplomacy and Negotiating Behavior: Emerging New Context for U.S. Diplomacy.* A study prepared by the Senior Specialists Division, Congressional Research Division, Library of Congress. Washington, D.C.: U.S. Government Printing Office, 1979.

U.S. Department of State, *Bulletin* and *Current Policy.* As cited in footnotes.

Other Books of Interest
from the Institute for the Study of Diplomacy and
University Press of America

CASE STUDIES IN DIPLOMACY

The Diplomacy of Human Rights
edited by David D. Newsom

U.N. Security Council Resolution 242: A Case Study in Diplomatic Ambiguity
by Lord Caradon, Arthur J. Goldberg, Mohamed El-Zayyat and Abba Eban

Resolution of the Dominican Crisis, 1965: A Study in Mediation
by Audrey Bracey, with concluding chapter by Martin F. Herz

Mediation of the West New Guinea Dispute, 1962: A Case Study
by Christopher J. McMullen, with Introduction by George C. McGhee

Resolution of the Yemen Crisis, 1963: A Case Study in Mediation
by Christopher J. McMullen

American Diplomats and the Franco-Prussian War: Perceptions from Paris and Berlin
by Patricia Dougherty, O.P.

Conference Diplomacy—A Case Study: The World Food Conference, Rome, 1974
by Edwin McC. Martin

Conference Diplomacy II—A Case Study: The UN Conference on Science and Technology for Development, Vienna, 1979
by Jean M. Wilkowski, with Foreword by John W. McDonald, Jr.

SYMPOSIA ON PROBLEMS AND PROCESSES OF DIPLOMACY

The Modern Ambassador: The Challenge and the Search
edited by Martin F. Herz, with Introduction by Ellsworth Bunker

Diplomats and Terrorists: What Works, What Doesn't—A Symposium
edited by Martin F. Herz

Contacts with the Opposition—A Symposium
edited by Martin F. Herz

The Role of Embassies in Promoting Business—A Symposium
edited by Martin F. Herz, with Overview by Theodore H. Moran

Diplomacy: The Role of the Wife—A Symposium
edited by Martin F. Herz

The Consular Dimension of Diplomacy—A Symposium
edited by Martin F. Herz

EXEMPLARY DIPLOMATIC REPORTING SERIES & OCCASIONAL PAPERS

David Bruce's "Long Telegram" of July 3, 1951
by Martin F. Herz

A View from Tehran: A Diplomatist Looks at the Shah's Regime in 1964
by Martin F. Herz

The North-South Dialogue and the United Nations
by John W. McDonald, Jr.

Making the World a Less Dangerous Place: Lessons Learned from a Career in Diplomacy
by Martin F. Herz

DIPLOMATIC AND CONTEMPORARY HISTORY

215 Days in the Life of an American Ambassador
by Martin F. Herz

First Line of Defense—Forty Years' Experiences of a Career Diplomat
by John Moors Cabot

The Vietnam War in Retrospect
by Martin F. Herz